Griffin's
Easy to Pronounce
Spanish

by
Cliff Davis

Griffin Publishing
Glendale, California

10 9 8 7 6 5 4 3 2 1

ISBN 1-882180-22-4

Griffin Publishing
544 Colorado Street
Glendale, California 91204

Telephone: 1-800-423-5789

Manufactured in the United States of America

INTRODUCTION

The EASY TO PRONOUNCE phrase book series has been developed with the conviction that learning to speak a foreign language should be fun and easy.

The EPLS Vowel Symbols is a unique phonetic system that stresses consistency, clarity and above all, simplicity! The basic Vowei Symbols have been placed on the back cover for easy reference.

You will be amazed at how confidence in your pronunciation will lead to an eagerness to talk to other people in their own language.

ACKNOWLEDGMENTS

The EASY TO PRONOUNCE LANGUAGE SYSTEM (EPLS) has been developed by Cliff Davis.

Series Editor
Richard D. Burns, Ph.D.

Series Associate Editor
Mark M. Dodge, M.A.

Spanish Language Consulting Editor
Ana-Lorena Richins M.

Book Design and Typeset
Regina Books, Claremont California.

Cover Design
Sylvia Hoffland, Long Beach, California.

Reviewers
Carol-Ann Jensen Fuller; Paul M. Richins, Cristina Silver, Carol and Ignacio Aguilar.

CONTENTS

PRONUNCIATION GUIDE

Most English speakers are familiar with the Spanish word **taco**. This is how its correct pronunciation is represented in this system.

This mark (´) above a symbol tells you to give it extra emphasis.

All vowel sounds are assigned a specific, non-changing symbol. When these symbols are used in conjunction with consonants and read normally, pronunciation of even the most difficult foreign word is incredibly EASY!!

On the following page you find all the symbols used in this book. The symbols are EASY to LEARN since their sounds are familiar. Beneath each symbol are three English words which contain the sound of the symbol.

THE SAME BASIC SYMBOLS ARE USED IN ALL EASY TO PRONOUNCE PHRASE BOOKS!

EPLS VOWEL SYMBOLS

(A)
Ace
Bake
Safe

(EE)
See
Green
Feet

(I)
Ice
Kite
Pie

(O)
Oak
Cold
Phone

(oo)
Cool
Pool
Too

(ĕ)
Pet
Red
Bed

(ah)
Off
Rock
Hot

(oy)
Toy
Boy
Joy

(ow)
Cow
How
Now

EPLS CONSONANTS

Consonants are letters like **T**, **D**, and **K**. They are easy to recognize and their pronunciation seldom changes. The following pronunciation guide letters represent some unique Spanish consonant sounds.

Ŗ represents a slightly rolled **r** sound.

Ŗ̣ represents a longer rolled **r** sound.

V represents the Spanish letter **v** and is pronounced like the **v** in vine but very softly. Depending on your location you will often hear the Spanish **v** pronounced like the **b** in boy.

B represents the Spanish letter **b** and sounds like the **b** in boy. Sometimes, the Spanish **b** is pronounced so softly the the lips barely touch. You must listen closely to a native speaker to master this sound.

PRONUNCIATION TIPS

- Each pronunciation guide word is broken into syllables. Read each word slowly, one syllable at a time, increasing speed as you become more familiar with the system.

- In Spanish it is important to stress certain syllables. This mark (´) over the syllable reminds you to stress that syllable.

- Most symbols are pronounced the way they look!

- It is estimated that nearly 300 million people now speak Spanish around the world. Don't be surprised to hear variations in the meanings and pronunciation of some Spanish words. The pronunciation and word choices in this book were chosen for their simplicity and effectiveness.

- In northern Spain, **z** before any letter and **c** before **e** or **i** is pronounced like the **th** in thin. In southern Spain and most of Latin America, **z** by itself or **c** before **e** or **i** sounds like an **s**. In this phrase book the **s** sound is used for **z** and **c** because of its wider usage throughout the Spanish speaking world.

ESSENTIAL WORDS AND PHRASES

Here are some basic words and phrases that will help you express your needs and feelings in Spanish.

Hello

Hola

ÓL-L(ah)

How are you?

¿Cómo está?

KÓ-MÓ (ĕ)S-T(ah)

Fine/ Very well

Muy bien

MW(ĒĒ) B(ĒĒ)-(ĕ)N

And you?

¿Y usted?

(ĒĒ) (oo)S-T(ĕ)D

Goodbye

Adiós

(ah)D-YÓS

Good morning

Buenos días

BWA-NOS DEE-ahS

Good evening

Buenas tardes

BWA-NahS TahR-DeS

Good night

Buenas noches

BWA-NahS NO-CHeS

Mr.

Señor

SAN-YOR

Mrs.

Señora

SAN-YO-Rah

Miss

Señorita

SAN-YO-REE-Tah

Yes

Sí

S**EE**

No

No

N**O**

Please

Por favor

P**O**R F**ah**-V**O**R

Abbreviated PFV throughout book

Thank you

Gracias

GR**ah**-S**EE**-**ah**S

Excuse me

Perdón   Discúlpe

P**ê**R-D**O**N   D**EE**S-K**oo**L-P**A**

Use **perdón** if you bump into someone and **discúlpe** to get one's attention.

I'm sorry

Lo siento

L**O** S**EE**-**ê**N-T**O**

I'm a tourist

Soy turista

Soy TOO-REES-Tah

I don't speak Spanish

No hablo español

NO ah-BLO eS-Pahn-YOL

Do you understand English?

¿Entiende inglés?

eN-TEE-eN-DA eN-GLAS

I don't understand!

¡No entiendo!

NO eN-TEE-eN-DO

Please repeat

Repita, por favor

RA-PEE-Tah PFV

I want...

Quiero...

KEE-e-RO...

I have...

Tengo...

TeN-GO...

I know

Yo sé

YO SA

I don't know

No sé

NO SA

I like it

Me gusta

MA GOO'S-Tah

I don't like it

No me gusta

NO MA GOO'S-Tah

I'm lost

Estoy perdido (male)
Estoy perdida (female)

eS-Toy' PeR-DEE'-DO

eS-Toy' PeR-DEE'-Dah

I'm in a hurry

Tengo prisa

TeN-GO PREE'-Sah

I'm tired

Estoy cansado (male)
Estoy cansada (female)

ĕS-Tⓞy̆ Kⓐ̄N-Sⓐ̄-Dⓞ
ĕS-Tⓞy̆ Kⓐ̄N-Sⓐ̄-Dⓐ̄

I'm late

Llegué tarde

Yⓐ-Gⓐ́ Tⓐ̄R-Dⓐ

You will notice that the Spanish letter **d** is somtimes pronounced with a **th** sound.

I'm hungry

Tengo hambre

Tĕ́N-Gⓞ ⓐ̄M-BRⓐ

I'm thirsty

Tengo sed

Tĕ́N-Gⓞ Sĕ̆D

My name is...

Me llamo...

MA Yah-MO...

What's your name?

¿Cómo se llama usted?

KO-MO SA Yah-Mah
ooS-TeD

Where are you from?

¿De dónde es usted?

DA DON-DA eS ooS-TeD

Do you live here?

¿Vive usted aquí?

VEE-VA ooS-TeD ah-KEE

I just arrived

Acabo de llegar

ah-Kah-BO DA YA-GahR

What hotel are you [staying] at?

¿En que hotel está usted?

eN KA O-TeL eS-Tah
ooS-TeD

I'm at the...hotel

Estoy en el hotel...

ⓔS-Tⓞⓨ́ ⓔN ⓔL ⓞ-Tⓔ́L...

It was nice to meet you

Mucho gusto

Mⓞⓞ́-CHⓞ Gⓞⓞ́S-Tⓞ

The pronunciation guide **G** is pronounced like the **g** in go.

See you later

Hasta luego

ⓐⓗ́S-Tⓐⓗ Lⓞⓞ-ⓐ́-Gⓞ

You will notice that in Spanish spelling the letter **e** is sometimes pronounced like the **e** in red and sometimes like the **a** in cake. This will vary from region to region and will not affect the understanding of the word.

THE BIG QUESTIONS

Who?

¿Quién?

K(EE)-(ě)N

Who is it?

¿Quién es?

K(EE)-(ě)N   (ě)S

What?

¿Qué?   ¿Cómo?

K(A)   K(O)-M(O)

Use ¿cómo? if you didn't hear well or want something repeated.

What's that?

¿Qué es eso?

K(A)   (ě)S   (ě)-S(O)

When?

¿Cuándo?

KW(ah)N-D(O)

Where?

¿Dónde?

D(O)N-D(A)

Where is...?

¿Dónde está...?

DÓN-DA ĕS-Tah...

Which?

¿Cuál?

KWahL

Why?

¿Por qué?

POB KA

How?

¿Cómo?

KÓ-MO

How much? (money)

¿Cuánto?

KWahN-TO

KW sounds like the **qu** in quit

How long?

¿Cuánto tiempo?

KWahN-TO TEE-ĕMPO

ASKING FOR THINGS

The following phrases are valuable when asking for directions, food or help, etc.

I would like...

Quisiera...

KⒺⒺ-SⒺⒺ-é-Rⓐⓗ...

I need...

Necesito...

NⒶ-SⒶ-SⒺⒺ-TⓄ...

Can you...

Puede usted...

PWⒶ-DⒶ ⓄⓄS-TéD...

Always remember to say please and thank you.

Please

Por favor

PⓄR Fⓐⓗ-VⓄR

Thank you

Gracias

GRⓐⓗ-SⒺⒺ-ⓐⓗS

PHRASEMAKER

Combine **I would like** with the following phrases beneath it and you will have a good idea how to ask for things.

I would like...

Quisiera...

KEE-SEE-ê-Rah...

more coffee

más café

MahS Kah-FA

some water

agua

ah-GWah

some ice

hielo

YA-LO

the menu

la carta

Lah KahR-Tah

PHRASEMAKER

Here are a few sentences you can use when you feel the urge to say I need...or can you?

I need...

Necesito...

N⒜-S⒜-SEE´-T⓪...

help

ayuda

⒜-Y⓪⓪´-D⒜

directions

direcciones

DEE-R⒠K-SEE-⓪´-N⒠S

more money

más dinero

M⒜S   DEE-N⒜´-R⓪

change

cambio

K⒜´M-BEE-⓪

a lawyer

un abogado

⓪⓪N   ⒜-B⓪-G⒜´-D⓪

Can you...
¿Puede usted...

PWA-DA ⓄⓄS-TⓔD...

help me?
ayudarme?

ⓐⒽ-YⓄⓄ-DⓐⒽR-MA

show me?
enseñarme?

ⓔN-SAN-YⓐⒽR-MA

give me...?
darme...?

DⓐⒽR-MA...

tell me...?
decirme...?

DA-SEER-MA...

take me to...?
llevarme al...?

YA-VⓐⒽR-MA ⓐⒽL...

ASKING THE WAY

No matter how independent you are, sooner or later you'll probably have to ask directions.

Where is...?

¿Dónde está...?

DÓN-D④ ⓔS-T⒜́...

Is it near?

¿Está cerca?

ⓔS-T⒜́ Sⓔ́R-K⒜

Is it far?

¿Está lejos?

ⓔS-T⒜́ L④́-Hⓞs

I'm lost!

¡Estoy perdido! (male)
¡Estoy perdida! (female)

ⓔS-Tⓞ⒴́ Pⓔ́R-DⒺⒺ́-Dⓞ

ⓔS-Tⓞ⒴́ Pⓔ́R-DⒺⒺ́-D⒜

I'm looking for...

Busco...

Bⓞⓞ́S-Kⓞ...

PHRASEMAKER

Where is...

¿Dónde está...

DÓN-DA ēS-Tah...

the restroom?

el baño?

ēL Bah-N-YO

the telephone?

el teléfono?

ēL TA-LA-FO-NO

the beach?

la playa?

Lah PLah-Yah

the hotel...?

el hotel...?

ēL O-TēL...

the train for...?

el tren para...?

ēL TREN Pah-Rah...

TIME

What time is it?

¿Qué hora es?

K(A)　(O)-R(ah)　(e)S

Morning

La mañana

L(ah)　M(ah)N-Y(ah)-N(ah)

Noon

El mediodía

(e)L　M(A)-D(EE)-(O)-D(EE)-(ah)

Night

La noche

L(ah)　N(O)-CH(A)

Today

Hoy

(oy)

In Spanish spelling the **h** is always silent.

Tomorrow

Mañana

M(ah)N-Y(ah)-N(ah)

This week
Esta semana
ĕS-Tah Sah-Mahʹ-Nah

This month
Este mes
ĕS-Tah MahS

This year
Este año
ĕS-Tah ahʹN-YO

Now
Ahora
ow-Oʹ-Rah

Soon
Pronto
PRONʹ-TO

Later
Más tarde
Mahs TahʹR-Dah

Never
Nunca
NooNʹ-Kah

WHO IS IT?

I
Yo
YⓄ

You (Formal)	**(Informal)**
Usted	Tú
ⓄⓄS-TⓔⓄD	TⓄⓄ
Use this form of **you** with people you don't know well	Use this form of **you** with people you know well

We

Nosotros	Nosotras
NⓄ-SⓄ́-TRⓄS	NⓄ-SⓄ́-TRⓐⓗS
A group of men only or a group of men & women	A group of women only

They

Ellos	Ellas
Ⓐ́-YⓄS	Ⓐ́-YⓐⓗS
A group of men only or a group of men & women	A group of women only

THE, A (AN), AND SOME

To use the correct form of The, **A (An)**, or **Some**, you must know if the Spanish word is masculine or feminine. Often you will have to guess! If you make a mistake, you will still be understood.

The

La

L(ah)

The before a singular feminine noun
(La) woman is pretty

Las

L(ah)S

The before a plural feminine noun
(Las) women are pretty

El

(e)L

The before a singular masculine noun
(El) man is handsome

Los

L(o)S

The before a plural masculine noun
(Los) men are handsome

A or An

Un

(oo)N

A or **an** before a singular masculine noun
He is (un) man

Una

(oo)-N(ah)

A or **an** before a singular feminine noun
She is (una) woman

Some

Unos

(oo)-N(o)S

Some before plural masculine nouns
(Unos) men

Unas

(oo)-N(ah)S

Some before plural feminine nouns
(Unas) women

USEFUL OPPOSITES

Near	**Far**
Cerca	Lejos
SĕR-Kah	LǼ-HOS

Here	**There**
Aquí	Ahí
ah-KEÉ	ah-EÉ

Left	**Right**
Izquierda	Derecha
EES-KEE-ĕR-Dah	DA-RA-CHah

A little	**A lot**
Un poquito	Mucho
ooN PO-KEÉ-TO	Moó-CHO

More	**Less**
Más	Menos
MahS	MǼ-NOS

Big	**Small**
Grande	Pequeño
GRahN-DA	PA-KǼN-YO

Opened

Abierto

@h-BEE-@R-T@

Closed

Cerrado

S@-B@h-D@

Cheap

Barato

B@h-B@h-T@

Expensive

Caro

K@h-R@

Clean

Limpio

L@M-P@-@

Dirty

Sucio

S@-S@-@

Good

Bueno

BW@-N@

Bad

Malo

M@h-L@

Vacant

Desocupado

D@-S@-K@-P@h-D@

Occupied

Ocupado

@-K@-P@h-D@

Right

Correcto

K@-B@K-T@

Wrong

Incorrecto

@N-K@-B@K-T@

WORDS OF ENDEARMENT

I love you

Te amo

T(A) (ah)-M(O)

My love

Mi amor

M(EE) (ah)-M(O)R

My life

Mi vida

M(EE) V(EE)-D(ah)

My friend (to a male)

Mi amigo

M(EE) (ah)-M(EE)-G(O)

My friend (to a female)

Mi amiga

M(EE) (ah)-M(EE)-G(ah)

Kiss me!

¡Bésame!

B(A)-S(ah)-M(A)

WORDS OF ANGER

What do you want?
¿Qué quiere usted?

KA KEE-ĕ-RA ⓄⓄS-TĕD

Leave me alone!
¡Déjeme en paz!

DÁ-HA-MA ĕN Pah S

Go away!
¡Vete!

VÁ-TA

Stop bothering me!
¡No me moleste más!

NⓄ MA MⓄ-LĕS-TA Mah S

Be Quiet!
¡Silencio!

SEE-LĕN-SEE-Ⓞ

That's enough!
¡Basta!

Bah S-Tah

COMMON EXPRESSIONS

When you are at a loss for words but have the feeling you should say something, try one of these!

Who knows?

¿Quién sabe?

KEE-ēN Sah-BA

That's the truth!

¡Es verdad!

ēS VēB-Dah'D

Sure!

¡Claro!

KLah'-BO

Wow!

¡Caramba!

Kah-Bah'M-Bah

What's happening?

¿Qué pasa?

KA Pah'-Sah

I think so!

¡Creo que sí!

KBA'-O KA SEE

Cheers!

¡Salud!

Sah-LOOD

Good luck!

¡Buena suerte!

BWA-Nah SWeR-TA

With pleasure!

¡Con mucho gusto!

KON MOO-CHO GOOS-TO

My goodness!

¡Diós mío!

DEE-OS MEE-O

What a shame or **Thats too bad!**

¡Qué lástima!

KA Lah-S-TEE-Mah

Well done! Bravo!

¡Olé!

O-LA

USEFUL COMMANDS

Stop!
¡Párese!
Pah-RA-SA

Go!
¡Vaya!
Vah-Yah

Wait!
¡Espérese!
eS-PA-RA-SA

Hurry!
¡Apurese!
ah-Poo-Re-SA

Slow down!
¡Despacio!
DA-SPah-SEE-O

Come here!
¡Venga acá!
VeN-Gah   ah-Kah

Help!
¡Socorro!
SO-KO-RO

Roll
the
R!

EMERGENCIES

Fire!

¡Incendio!

EEN-SěN-DEE-O

Emergency!

¡Emergencia!

A-MěR-HěN-SEE-ah

Call the police!

¡Lláme al policia!

Yah-MA ahL PO-LEE-SEE-ah

Call a doctor!

¡Lláme a un médico!

Yah-MA ah ooN MA-DEE-KO

Call an ambulance!

¡Lláme una ambulancia!

Yah-MA oo-Nah ahM-Boo-LahN-SEE-ah

I need help!

¡Necesito ayuda!

NA-SA-SEE-TO ah-Yoo-Dah

ARRIVAL

Passing through customs should be easy since there are usually agents available who speak English. You may be asked how long you intend to stay and if you have anything to declare.

- Have your passport ready.

- Be sure all documents are up to date.

- While in a foreign country, it is wise to keep receipts for everything you buy.

- Be aware that many countries will charge a departure tax when you leave. Your travel agent should be able to find out if this affects you.

- If you have connecting flights, be sure to reconfirm them in advance.

- Make sure your luggage is clearly marked inside and out.

- Take valuables and medicines in carry on bags.

SIGNS TO LOOK FOR:

ADUANA (CUSTOMS)

FRONTERA (BORDER)

CONTROL DE EQUIPAJE (BAGGAGE CONTROL)

EQUIPAJE PERDIDO (LOST BAGGAGE)

KEY WORDS

Baggage

El equipaje

ⓔL Ⓐ-KⒺ-Pⓐʰ-HⒶ

Customs

La aduana

Lⓐʰ ⓐʰ-DWⓐʰ-Nⓐʰ

Documents

Los documentos

LⓄS DⓄ-Kⓞⓞ-MⓔN-TⓄS

Passport

El pasaporte

ⓔL Pⓐʰ-Sⓐʰ-PⓄʳB-TⒶ

Porter

El maletero   El mozo (Spain)

ⓔL Mⓐʰ-LⒶ-TⒶ-BⓄ

ⓔL MⓄ-THⓄ

Notice that in Spain the letter **z** is prounounced as **th**.

Tax

Los impuestos

LⓄS ⒺM-PWⓔS-TⓄS

USEFUL PHRASES

I have nothing to declare

No tengo nada que declarar

NO TEN-GO Nah-Dah KA
DA-KLah-RahR

I'll be staying...

Me voy a quedar...

 MA Voy ah KA-DahR...

one week

una semana

OO-Nah SA-Mah-Nah

two weeks

dos semanas

DOS SA-Mah-NahS

one month

un mes

OON MAS

two months

dos meses

DOS MAS-eS

I'm here on business

Vengo de negocios

VéN-GO DA NA-GÓ-SEE-OS

I'm here on vacation

Vengo de vacaciones

VéN-GO DA

Vah-Kah-SEE-Ó-NéS

Here is my passport

Aquí tiene mi pasaporte

ah-KEÉ TEE-é-NA MEE

Pah-Sah-PÓR-TA

Is there a problem?

¿Hay algún problema?

I ahL-GOÓN PRO-BLA-Mah

I don't understand

No comprendo

NO KOM-PRéN-DO

Do you speak English?

¿Habla usted inglés?

ah-BLah ooS-TéD EEN-GLA'S

PHRASEMAKER

Where is...

¿Dónde está...

DON-DA eS-Tah...

customs?

la aduana?

Lah ah-DWah-Nah

baggage claim?

el equipaje?

eL A-KEE-Pah-HA

the money exchange?

la casa de cambio?

Lah Kah-Sah DA KahM-BEE-O

the taxi stand?

la parada de taxis?

Lah Pah-Rah-Dah DA TahK-SEES

the bus stop?

la parada de autobuses?

Lah Pah-Rah-Dah DA
ow-TO-Boo-SeS

I need a porter!

Necesito un maletero!

NA-SA-SÉE-TO OON
MAH-LA-TA-RO

These are my bags

Estas son mis maletas

ĔS-TAHS SON MEES
MAH-LA-TAHS

I'm missing a bag

Me falta una maleta

MA FAHL-TAH OO-NAH
MAH-LA-TAH

Take my bags to a taxi please

Lléve mis maletas al taxi por favor

YA-VA MEES MAH-LA-TAHS AHL
TAHK-SEE PFV

Thank you. This is for you

Gracias. Esto es para usted

GRAH-SEE-AHS ĔS-TO ĔS
PAH-RAH OOS-TĔD

HOTEL SURVIVAL

A wide variety of accommodations, ranging from the most basic to the most extravagant, are available wherever you travel. When booking your room, find out what amenities are included for the price you pay.

- Make reservations well in advance and get written confirmation of reservation before you leave home.

- Always have identification ready when checking in.

- Hotels in some foreign countries may require you to hand over your passport when checking in. It is usually returned the next day.

- Do not leave valuables, prescriptions or cash in your room when you are not there!

- Electrical items like blow dryers may need an adaptor. Your hotel may be able to provide one, but to be safe take one with you.

- Although a service charge is usually included on your bill, it is customary to tip maids, bellhops, and doorman.

KEY WORDS

Hotel
El hotel

ẽL Ⓞ-Tẽ́L

Bellman
El botones

ẽL BⓄ-TⓄ́-Nẽ́S

Maid
La criada

Lⓐ KRⒺ-ⓐ́-Dⓐ

Message
El recado

ẽL RⒶ-Kⓐ́-DⓄ

Reservation
La reservación

Lⓐ RⒶ-Sẽ́R-Vⓐ-SⒺ-Ó́N

Room service
El servicio de habitación

ẽL Sẽ́R-VⒺ́-SⒺ-Ⓞ DⒶ

ⓐ-BⒺ-Tⓐ-SⒺ-Ó́N

CHECKING IN

My name is...

Me llamo...

MA Yah-MO...

I have a reservation

Tengo una reserva

TĕN-GO oo-Nah RA-SĕR-Vah

If you don't have a reservation, just say **no** before this phrase

Have you any vacancies?

¿Tiene alguna habitación libre?

TEE-ĕ-NA ahL-GOO-Nah
ah-BEE-Tah-SEE-ON LEE-BRA

What is the charge per night?

¿Cuánto es por noche?

KWahN-TO ĕS POR NO-CHA

Is there room service?

¿Hay servicio de habitación?

I SĕR-VEE-SEE-O DA
ah-BEE-Tah-SEE-ON

I would like a room with...

Quisiera un cuarto con...

KEE-SEE-é-Rah oON KWah'R-TO KON...

a bath

un baño

ooN Bah'N-YO

a shower

una ducha

oo'-Nah Doo'-CHah

one bed

una cama

oo'-Nah Kah'-Mah

two beds

dos camas

DOS Kah'-Mahs

a view

una vista

oo'-Nah VEE'S-Tah

USEFUL PHRASES

Where is the dining room?

¿Dónde está el comedor?

DÓN-DA̐ ĕS-Táh

ĕL KŌ-MA̐-DŌR

Are meals included?

¿Están las comidas incluidas?

ĕS-TáhN Lah̐S KŌ-MĒ-Dah̐S

ĒN-KLōō-Ē-Dah̐S

What time is...

¿A qué hora es...

ah̐ KA̐ Ō-Rah̐ ĕS...

breakfast?

el desayuno?

ĕL DĕS-ah̐-Yōō-NŌ

lunch?

la comida?

Lah̐ KŌ-MĒ-Dah̐

dinner?

la cena?

Lah̐ SA̐-Nah̐

My room key, please

La llave de mi cuarto, por favor

L(ah) Y(ah)-V(A) D(A) M(EE)
KW(ah)R-T(O) PFV

Are there any messages for me?

¿Tengo algún recado?

T(e)N-G(O) (ah)L-G(oo)N R(A)-K(ah)-D(O)

Please wake me at...

Me despierte a las...

↓ M(A) D(e)S-P(EE)-(e)R-T(A) (ah) L(ah)S...

6:00	6:30
seis	seis y media
S(A)S	S(A)S (EE) M(A)-D(EE)-(ah)

7:00	7:30
siete	siete y media
S(EE)-(e)-T(A)	S(EE)-(e)-T(A) (EE) M(A)-D(EE)-(ah)

8:00	8:30
ocho	ocho y media
(O)-CH(O)	(O)-CH(O) (EE) M(A)-D(EE)-(ah)

9:00	9:30
nueve	nueve y media
NW(e)-V(A)	NW(e)-V(A) (EE) M(A)-D(EE)-(ah)

PHRASEMAKER

I need...

Necesito...

↓ N(A)-S(A)-S(EE)-T(O)...

---

soap

jabón

H(ah)-B(O)N

---

more towels

más toallas

M(ah)S   TW(ah)-Y(ah)S

---

ice cubes

cubitos de hielo

K(oo)-B(EE)-T(O)S   D(A)   Y(A)-L(O)

---

toilet paper

papel higiénico

P(ah)-P(ĕ)L   (EE)-H(EE)-(ĕ)-N(EE)-K(O)

---

a bellman

un botones

(oo)N   B(O)-T(O)-N(ĕ)S

↓

a maid
una criada
 oo-Nah KREE-ah-Dah

the manager
el gerente
eL HA-ReN-TA

a babysitter
una niñera
oo-Nah NEEN-YA-Bah

an extra key
otra llave
O-TRah Yah-VA

a hotel safe
una caja fuerte
oo-Nah Kah-Hah FWeR-TA

clean sheets
sábanas limpias
Sah-Bah-NahS LEEM-PEE-ahS

more blankets
mas cobijas (mantas)
MahS KO-BEE-HahS (MahN-TahS)

PHRASEMAKER

(PROBLEMS)

There is no...

No hay...

N◉ ①...

---

hot water

agua caliente

ⓐ́-GWⓐ Kⓐ-Lㄸ-ⓔ́N-Tⓐ

---

heat

calefacción

Kⓐ-Lⓐ-Fⓐ́K-Sㄸ-Ó́N

---

light

luz

L⬤S

---

electricity

electricidad

Ⓐ-Lⓔ̈K-TRㄸ-Sㄸ-Dⓐ́D

---

toilet paper

papel higiénico

Pⓐ-Pⓔ̈́L ㄸ-Hㄸ-ⓔ̈́-Nㄸ-K◉

PHRASEMAKER
(SPECIAL NEEDS)

Do you have...

¿Tiene...

T(EE)-(e)-N(A)...

facilities for the disabled?

facilidades para los inválidos?

F(ah)-S(EE)-L(EE)-D(ah)-D(e)S   P(ah)-R(ah)
L(O)S   (EE)N-V(ah)-L(EE)-D(O)S

a wheel chair?

una silla de ruedas?

(oo)-N(ah)   S(EE)-Y(ah)   D(A)   R(oo)-(A)-D(ah)S

an elevator?

un ascensor?

(OO)N   (ah)-S(e)N-S(O)R

a ramp?

una rampa?

(oo)-N(ah)   R(ah)M-P(ah)

CHECKING OUT

The bill please

La cuenta por favor

L@h KW@N-T@h PFV

Is this bill correct?

¿Está bien la cuenta?

@S-T@h B@-@N L@h KW@N-T@h

Do you accept credit cards?

¿Se acepta tarjetas de crédito?

S@ @h-S@P-T@h T@hR-H@-T@hS
D@ KR@-D@-T@

Could you have my luggage brought down?

¿Pueden bajarme el equipaje?

PW@-D@N B@h-H@hR-M@ @L
@-K@-P@h-H@

Can you call a taxi for me?

¿Puede llamarme un taxi?

PW@-D@ Y@h-M@hR-M@ @N
T@hK-S@

I had a very good time!

¡Me lo pasé muy bien!

MA LO Pah-SA MWEE BEE-eN

Thanks for everything

Gracias por todo

GRah-SEE-ahS POR TO-DO

We'll see you next time

Nos veremos la próxima!

NOS Ve-RA-MOS
Lah PROK-SEE-Mah

Goodbye

Adiós

ahD-YOS

RESTAURANT SURVIVAL

The food available in Latin America and Spain is diverse. You will find a variety of tasty regional specialties. Meal times may be quite different than what you are used to!

- In Latin America and Spain, breakfast is usually served till 11 AM, lunch between 1 and 4 PM, and dinner from 8 PM till midnight. These are general guidelines and vary from country to country.

- Breakfast is usually continental. Lunch is the largest and most complete meal of the day. In the evening a snack or small meal is served.

- A tip or service charge is often automatically included in your bill. Look for the words **SERVICIO INCLUIDO**.

SIGNS TO LOOK FOR:

CANTINA (BAR)
HACIENDA (RANCH STYLE)
RESTAURANTE (TRADITIONAL)

(IN SPAIN)
TASCA (BAR)
CAFE (SNACKS)
RESTAURANTE (TRADITIONAL)

KEY WORDS

Breakfast

El desayuno

ⓔL DⓔS-ⓐ-Yⓞⓞ-Nⓞ

Lunch

El almuerzo

ⓔL ⓐL-MWⓔB-Sⓞ

Dinner

La cena

Lⓐ S④'-Nⓐ

Waiter

El camarero

ⓔL Kⓐ-Mⓐ-B④'-Bⓞ

Waitress

La camarera

Lⓐ Kⓐ-Mⓐ-B④'-Bⓐ

Restaurant

El restaurante

ⓔL BⓔS-Tⓞⓦ-Bⓐ'N-T④

USEFUL PHRASES

A table for...

Una mesa para...

↓ OO-Nah MA-Sah Pah-Rah...

2	4	6
dos	cuatro	seis
DOS	KWah-TRO	SAS

The menu please

La carta por favor

Lah Kah-B-Tah PFV

Separate checks please

Cuentas separadas por favor

KWeN-Tahs SA-Pah-Rah-Dahs PFV

We are in a hurry

Tenemos prisa

Te-NA-MOS PREE-Sah

What do you recommend?

¿Qué se recomienda la casa?

KA SA RA-KO-MEE-eN-Dah

Lah Kah-Sah

Prease bring me...

Traigame... por favor

TRĪ-G@h-M@...PFV

Please bring us...

Triagnos... por favor

TRĪ-G@h-N©S...PFV

I'm hungry

Tengo hambre

Tế-N-G© @h́M-BR@

I'm thirsty

Tengo sed

Tế-N-G© Sế-D

Is service included?

¿Está incluido el servicio?

ế-S-T@h́ EE-N-KL©©-EE-D©

ế-L Sế-R-VEế-SEE-©

The bill please

La cuenta por favor

L@h KWế-N-T@h PFV

ORDERING BEVERAGES

Ordering beverages is easy and a great way to practice your Spanish! Remember you may have to request ice with your drinks.

Please bring me...

Traígame por favor...

TRⒾ-Gⓐⓗ-Mⓐ PFV...

coffee	**tea**
el café	el té
ⒺL Kⓐⓗ-FⒶ	ⒺL Tⓐ

with cream

con crema

KⓄN KRⒶ-Mⓐⓗ

with sugar

con azúcar

KⓄN ⓐⓗ-SⓄⓄ-KⓐⓗR

with lemon

con limón

KⓄN LⒺⒺ-MⓄN

with ice

con hielo

KⓄN Yⓐ-LⓄ

Soft drinks

Los refrescos

LOS BA-FRĕS-KOS

Milk

La leche

Lah LA-CHA

Hot chocolate

El chocolate

ĕL CHO-KO-Lah-TA

Juice

El jugo

ĕL HOO-GO

Orange juice

El jugo de naranja

ĕL HOO-GO DA Nah-Bah'N-Hah

Ice water

El agua fría

ĕL ah-GWah FRĔE-ah

Mineral water

El agua mineral

ĕL ah-GWah MĔE-NA-Bah'L

AT THE BAR

Bartender

El cantinero

ⓔL KⓐN-TⒺ-NⒶ́-Ⓡ0

The wine list please

La lista de vinos por favor

LⓐH LⒺ́S-TⓐH DⒶ VⒺ́-N0S PFV

Cocktail

El coctél

ⓔL Kⓞ́K-TⓔL

On the rocks

Con hielo

K0N YⒶ́-L0

Straight

Sin hielo

SⒺN YⒶ́-L0

With lemon

con limón

K0N LⒺ-Mⓞ́N

PHRASEMAKER

I would like a glass of...

Quisiera un vaso de...

KEE-SEE-ĕ́-Rah   ooN

Vah́-SO   DA...

champagne

champaña

CHahM-Pah́N-Yah

beer

cerveza

Sĕ́R-VÁ-Sah

wine

vino

VEE-́NO   or   BEE-́NO

You will often hear the Spanish letter **v** pronounced
like a soft English **b**

red wine

vino tinto

VEE-́NO   TEÉN-TO

white wine

vino blanco

VEE-́NO   BLah́N-KO

ORDERING BREAKFAST

In Latin America, breakfast can be extravagant. In Spain, breakfast is generally a simple meal consisting of coffee or tea and bread.

Bread

El pan

ⒺL PⓐN

Toast...

El pan tostado...

↓ ⒺL PⓐN TⓄ-STⓐ-DⓄ...

with butter

con mantequilla

KⓄN MⓐN-TⒶ-KⒺⒺ-Yⓐ

with jam

con mamelada

KⓄN MⓐB-MⒶ-Lⓐ-Dⓐ

Cereal

El cereal

ⒺL SⒶ-BⒶ-ⓐL

PHRASEMAKER

I would like...

Quisiera...

KEE-SEE-é-Rah...

two eggs...

dos huevos...

DOS WA-VOS...

with bacon

con tocino

KON TO-SEE-NO

with ham

con jamón

KON Hah-MON

with potatoes

con papas   con patatas (Spain)

KON Pah-PahS   KON Pah-Tah-TahS

HOW DO YOU WANT YOUR EGGS?

Scrambled   **Fried**

Revueltos   Fritos

RA-VWéL-TOS   FREE-TOS

LUNCH AND DINNER

Although you are encouraged to sample regional cuisines, it is important to be able to order foods you are familiar with. This section will provide words and phrases to help you.

I would like...

Quiseiera...

KEE-SEE-ě-Rah...

We would like...

Quisiéramos...

KEE-SEE-ě-Rah-MOS...

Bring us...

Traíganos...

TRĪ-Gah-NOS...

The lady would like...

La señora quisiera...

Lah SAN-YO-Rah KEE-SEE-ě-Rah...

The gentleman would like...

El señor quisiera...

ěL SAN-YOR KEE-SEE-ě-Rah...

STARTERS

Appetizers

Los entremeses

LOS ĕN-TRĀ-MĀ-SĕS

Bread and butter

El pan y la mantequilla

ĕL PahN EE Lah
MahN-TĀ-KEE-Yah

Cheese

El queso

ĕL KĀ-SO

Fruit

La fruta

Lah FRoo-Tah

Salad

La ensalada

Lah ĕN-Sah-Lah-Dah

Soup

La sopa

Lah SO-Pah

MEATS

Beef

La carne de res

L@ K@R-N@ D@ R@S

Beef Steak

El bistec

@L B@-ST@K

Pork

La carne de puerco   Las carnitas (Mexico)

L@ K@R-N@ D@ PW@R-K@

L@S K@R-N@-T@S

Ham

El jamón

@L H@-M@N

Bacon

El tocino

@L T@-S@-N@

Lamb

El cordero

@L K@R-D@-R@

Veal

La carne de ternera

L@ K@R-N@ D@ T@R-N@-R@

POULTRY

Baked chicken

El pollo al horno

ⓔL PⓄ́-YⓄ ⓐL Ⓞ́R-NⓄ

Broiled chicken

El pollo a la parrilla

ⓔL PⓄ́-YⓄ ⓐ Lⓐ Pⓐ-Bⓔ́Ⓔ-Yⓐ

Fried chicken

El pollo frito

ⓔL PⓄ́-YⓄ FRⓔ́Ⓔ-TⓄ

Duck

El pato

ⓔL Pⓐ́-TⓄ

Turkey

El pavo   or   El guajolote (Mexico)

ⓔL Pⓐ́-VⓄ

ⓔL GWⓐ-HⓄ-LⓄ́-Tⓐ

Goose

El ganso

ⓔL Gⓐ́N-SⓄ

SEAFOOD

Fish

El pescado

ĕL PĕS-Kah-DO

Lobster

La langosta

Lah Lah-N-GO-STah

Oysters

Las ostras

Lah-S O-S-TRah-S

Salmon

El salmón

ĕL Sah-L-MO-N

Shrimp

Los camarones

LOS Kah-Mah-RO-NĕS

Trout

La trucha

Lah TROO-CHah

Tuna

El atún

ĕL ah-TOO-N

OTHER ENTREES

Sandwich

La torta (Latin America)   El bocadillo (Spain)

Lah TOR-Tah

eL BO-Kah-DEE-YO

Hot dog

El hot dog

eL Hah T Dah G

Hamburger

La hamburguesa

Lah ah M-BooB-GA-Sah

French fries

Las papas fritas or Las patatas fritas

Lah S Pah-Pah S FBEE-Tah S

Lah S Pah-Tah-Tah S FBEE-Tah S

Pasta

La pasta

Lah Pah S-Tah

Pizza

La pizza

Lah PEE T-Sah

VEGETABLES

Carrots

Las zanahorias

L**ah**S   S**ah**-N**O**́-R**EE**-**ah**S

Corn

El maiz

ĕL   M**ah**-**EE**́S

Mushrooms

Los hongos   Los champiñones (Spain)

L**O**S   **O**́N-G**O**S   L**O**S   CH**ah**M-P**EE**N-Y**O**́-N**A**S

Onions

Las cebollas

L**ah**S   S**A**-B**O**́-Y**ah**S

Potato

La papa   La patata (Spain)

L**ah**   P**ah**́-P**ah**   L**ah**   P**ah**-T**ah**́-T**ah**

Rice

El arróz

ĕL   **ah**-R**O**́S

Tomato

El tomate   el jitomate

ĕL   T**O**-M**ah**́-T**A**   **ĕ**L   H**EE**-T**O**-M**ah**́-T**A**

FRUITS

Apple
La manzana
Lah Mahn-Sah-Nah

Banana
La banana
Lah Bah-Nah-Nah

Grapes
Las uvas
LahS oo-VahS

Lemon
El limón
eL Lee-MoN

Orange
La naranja
Lah Nah-Rahn-Hah

Strawberry
La fresa
Lah FRa-Sah

Watermelon
La sandia
Lah SahN-Dee-ah

DESSERT

Desserts
Los Postres
LOS POS-TRёS

Apple pie
El pastel de manzana
ёL Pah-STёL DA MahN-Sah-Nah

Cherry pie
El pastel de cereza
ёL Pah-STёL DA SA-RA-Sah

Pastries
Los pasteles
LOS Pah-STё-LёS

Candy
Los dulces
LOS DooL-SёS

Ice cream
La nieve
El helado (Spain)

La NEE-A-VA

ёL A-Lah-DO

Ice cream cone
El barquillo de helado

ⓔL BⓐḨ-Kⓔⓔ-Yⓞ Dⓐ ⓐ-Lⓐḧ-Dⓞ

Chocolate
El chocolate

ⓔL CHⓞ-Kⓞ-Lⓐḧ-Tⓐ

Strawberry
La fresa

Lⓐ FḦⓐ-Sⓐ

Vanilla
La vanilla

Lⓐ Vⓘ-Nⓔⓔ-Yⓐ

CONDIMENTS

Salt
La sal

Lah Sahl

Pepper
La pimienta

Lah PEE-MEE-ĕN-Tah

Sugar
El azúcar

ĕL ah-SOO-Kahr

Mayonnaise
La mayonesa

Lah Mah-YO-NA-Sah

Butter
La mantequilla

Lah Mahn-TA-KEE-Yah

Mustard
La mostaza

Lah MOS-Tah-Sah

Ketchup
El ketchup

ĕL Kĕ-CHOOP

Vinegar and oil
El vinagre y aceite

ĕL VEE-Nah-GRA EE ah-SA-TA

SETTINGS

A cup
Una tasa
ōō´-Nah Tah´-Sah

A glass
Un vaso
ōōN Vah´-Sō

A spoon
Una cuchara
ōō´-Nah Kōō-CHah´-Rah

A fork
Un tenedor
ōōN Tē-Nā-DŌ´R

A knife
Un cuchillo
ōōN Kōō-CHēē´-Yō

A plate
Un plato
ōōN PLah´-Tō

A napkin
Una servieta
ōō´-Nah Sē̆R-Vēē-ē̆´-Tah

HOW DO YOU WANT IT COOKED?

Baked

Al horno

@hL O'R-NO

Broiled

a la parrilla

Roll the R!

@h L@h P@h-R@EE'-Y@h

Steamed

al vapor

@hL V@h-PO'R

Fried

Frito

FR@EE'-TO

Rare

Poco cocida

PO'-KO KO-S@EE'-D@h

Medium

Termino médio

T@ë'R-M@EE-NO M@A'-D@EE-O

Well done

Bien cocida

B@EE-@ë'N KO-S@EE'-D@h

PROBLEMS

I didn't order this

No pedí esto

NO P⒜-DEE ⒠S-TO

Is the bill correct?

¿Está bien la cuenta?

⒠S-T⒜ BEE-⒠N L⒜ KW⒠N-T⒜

Bring me...

Traígame...

↓ TRⒾ-G⒜-M⒜...

another spoon please

otra cuchara por favor

O-TR⒜ Koo-CH⒜-R⒜ PFV

another fork please

otro tenedor por favor

O-TRO T⒠-N⒜-DOR PFV

another plate please

otro plato por favor

O-TRO PL⒜-TO PFV

GETTING AROUND

Getting around in a foreign country can be an adventure in itself!

Taxi and bus drivers do not always speak English, so it is essential to be able to give simple directions. Most large cities in Latin America and Spain have efficient subway systems which provide an inexpensive way to tour the city. The words and phrases in this chapter will help you get where you're going.

- Negotiate the fare with your taxi driver in advance so there are no misunderstandings. Tell him where you want to go and find out exactly what he intends to charge.

- Never get in unmarked taxi cabs no matter where you are!

- Check with your travel agent about special rail passes which allow unlimited travel within a set period of time.

- If you are traveling by train in Europe, remember trains leave on time. Arrive early to allow time for ticket purchasing and checking in.

- Most towns have an office of tourism where you can pick up bus schedules printed in English.

KEY WORDS

Airport (See page 82)

El aeropuerto

ⓔL Ⓘ-Ⓡ◎-PWⓔ̈Ⓡ-T◎

Bus Station / Stop (See page 84)

La estación de autobuses
La parada de autobuses

Lⓐⓗ ⓔ-STⓐⓗ-Sㄹ-ⓄN DⒶ ⓌTⓄ-Ⓑ◎◎́-Sⓔ̈S
Lⓐⓗ Pⓐⓗ-Ⓡⓐⓗ́-Dⓐⓗ DⒶ ⓌTⓄ-Ⓑ◎◎́-Sⓔ̈S

Car Rental Agency (See page 86)

Una agencia de carros / aquilados

◎◎N-ⓐⓗ ⓐⓗ-Hⓔ̈N-Sㄹ-ⓐⓗ DⒶ
Kⓐⓗ́-Ⓡ◎S / ⓐⓗ-Kㄹ-Lⓐⓗ́-D◎S

Subway Station (See page 88)

La estación de metro

Lⓐⓗ ⓔ-STⓐⓗ-Sㄹ-ⓄN DⒶ MⒶ́-TⒺ◎

Taxi Stand (See page 90)

La parada de taxis

ⓔL Tⓐⓗ́K-Sㄹ

Train Station (See page 88)

La estación de ferrocarilles

Lⓐⓗ ⓔ-STⓐⓗ-Sㄹ-ⓄN DⒶ
FⒶ-Ⓡ◎-Kⓐⓗ-Ⓡㄹ́L-ⓔ̈S

AIR TRAVEL

Arrivals

Las llegadas

L@S Y@-G@-D@S

Departures

Las salidas

L@S S@-L@-D@S

Flight number...

El numero de vuelo...

@L N@-M@-R@ D@ VW@-L@...

Airline

La línea aérea

L@ L@-N@-Y@ @-@-R@-@

The gate

La puerta

L@ PW@R-T@

Information

Información

@N-F@R-M@-S@-@N

Ticket (airline)

El boleto

@L B@-L@-T@

Reservations

Las reservaciónes

L@S R@-S@R-V@-S@-@-N@S

Note: See arrival section for phrases on baggage

I would like a seat...

Quisiera un asiento...

KEE-SEE-é-Rah ooN ah-SEE-éN-TO...

in the no smoking section

en la sección de no fumar

éN Lah SéK-SEE-óN Dā NO Foo-MahR

next to the window

cerca de la ventana

SéR-Kah Dā Lah VéN-Tah-Nah

on the aisle

en el pasillo

éN éL Pah-SEE-YO

near the exit

cerca de la salida

SéR-Kah Dā Lah Sah-LEE-Dah

in first class

en la sección de primera clase

éN Lah SéK-SEE-óN Dā PREE-MĀ-Rah KLah-SĀ

THE BUS

Bus

El autobús   or   el camión (Mexico)

ĕL ōw-TO-BōōS   ĕL Kah-MEE-ON

Where is the bus stop?

¿Dónde está la parada de autobuses?

DON-DA ĕS-Tah Lah
Pah-Rah-Dah DA ōw-TO-Bōō-SĕS

Do you go to...?

¿Va usted a...?

Vah ōō-STĕD ah...

What is the fare?

¿Cuál es la tarifa?

KWahL ĕS Lah Tah-REE-Fah

Do I need exact change?

¿Necesito tener cambio exacto?

NA-SA-SEE-TO Tĕ-NĕR
KahM-BEE-O ĕK-SahK-TO

How often do the buses run?

¿Cada cuándo pasan los autobuses?

Kah-Dah KWahN-DO Pah-SahN
LOS ōw-TO-Bōō-SĕS

PHRASEMAKER

Please tell me...

Dígame por favor...

DEE-Gah-MA PFV...

which bus goes to...

cuál autobús va para...

KWah L ow-TO-Boo'S Vah Pah-Rah...

at what time does the bus leave

a que hora sale el autobús

ah KA O'-Rah Sah-LA eL ow-TO-Boo'S

where the bus stop is

dónde esta la parada de autobuses

DO'N-DA eS-Tah Lah

Pah-Rah-Dah DA ow-TO-Boo-SeS

when we are at...

cuando estamos en...

KWah'N-DO eS-Tah'-MOS eN...

where to get off

dónde debo bajarme?

DO'N-DA DA'-BO Bah-Hah'R-MA

BY CAR

Fill it up

Llénelo

YÉ-NA-LO

Please check...

Revise...

↓ RA-VEE-SA...

the oil

el aceite por favor

ÉL ah-SA-TA PFV

the battery

la batería por favor

Lah Bah-TA-REE-ah PFV

the tires

las llantas por favor

Lah S Yah N-Tah S PFV

the water

el agua por favor

ÉL ah-GWah PFV

the brakes

los frenos

LOS FRA-NOS

Can you help me?

¿Puede usted ayudarme?

PWA-DA ooS-TeD ah-Yoo-DahR-MA

My car won't start

Mi carro no arranca

MEE Kah-RO NO ah-RahN-Kah

I need a mechanic

Necesito un mecánico

NA-SA-SEE-TO ooN
MA-Kah-NEE-KO

Can you fix it?

¿Pueden arreglarlo?

PWA-DeN ah-RA-GLahR-LO

What will it cost?

¿Cuánto costará?

KWahN-TO KO-STah-Rah

That's too expensive

¡Es demasiado!

eS DEE-Mah-SEE-ah-DO

How long will it take?

¿Cuánto tiempo dura?

KWahN-TO TEE-eM-PO Doo-Rah

SUBWAYS AND TRAINS

Where is the subway station?

¿Dónde está el metro?

DON-DA eS-Tah eL MA-TRO

Where is the train station?

¿Dónde está la estación de ferrocarril?

DON-DA eS-Tah Lah eS-Tah-
SEE-ON DA FA-RO-Kah-REEL

A one way ticket please

Un billete de ida por favor

ooN BEE-YA-TA DA EE-Dah   PFV

A round trip ticket

Un billete de ida y vuelta

ooN BEE-YA-TA DA EE-Dah EE
VWeL-Tah PFV

First class

Primera clase

PREE-MA-Rah KLah-SA

Second class

Segundaclase

SA-GooN-Dah KLah-SA

Which train do I take to go to...?

¿Cuál tren tomo para ir a...?

KW@L TR͡EN TO͠-MO
P@-R@ EER @...

What is the fare?

¿Cuánto es la pasaje?

KW@N-TO͠ ēS L@ P@-S@-H@

Is this seat taken?

¿Está ocupado este asiento?

ēS-T@ O͠-KOO-P@-DO
ēS-T@ @-SEE-ēN-TO͠

Do I have to change trains?

¿Tengo que cambiar el tren?

TēN-GO͠ K@ K@M-BEE-@R
ēL TR͡EN

Does this train stop at...?

¿Se para este tren en...?

S@ P@-R@ ēS-T@ TR͡EN ēN...

Where are we?

¿Dónde estamos?

DO͠N-D@ ēS-T@-MOS

TAXI

Can you call a taxi for me?

¿Me puede llamar un taxi?

MⒶ PWⒶ́-DⒶ Yⓐⓗ-Mⓐⓗ́R ⓄⓄN
Tⓐⓗ́K-SⒺⒺ

Are you available?

¿Está usted libre?

ⓔS-Tⓐⓗ́ ⓄⓄS-TⓔD LⒺⒺ́-BRⒶ

I want to go...

Quiero ir ...

KⒺⒺ-ⓔ́-RⓄ ⒺⒺR...

Stop here please

Pare aquí por favor

Pⓐⓗ́-RⒶ ⓐⓗ-KⒺⒺ́ PFV

Please wait

Espérese por favor

ⓔ-SPⓔ́-RⒶ-SⒶ PFV

How much do I owe?

¿Cuánto le debo?

KWⓐⓗ́N-TⓄ LⒶ DⒶ́-BⓄ

PHRASEMAKER

I would like to go...

Quisiera ir...

KEE-SEE-ě-Rah EER...

to the hotel...

al hotel...

ahL O-TěL...

to this address

a ésta dirección

ah ěS-Tah DEE-RěK-SEE-ÓN

to the airport

al aeropuerto

ahL I-RO-PWěR-TO

to the subway station

al metro

ahL MÁ-TRO

to the hospital

al hospital

ah OS-PEE-TahL

SHOPPING

Whether you plan a major shopping spree or just need to purchase some basic necessities, the following information is useful.

- In Latin America and Spain, shops generally close in the afternoon for siesta . They reopen in the late afternoon and stay open into the night.

- You are likely to encounter an item called VAT (in Mexico IVA). This stands for Value Added Tax.

  It is a tax which is added to the price of all merchandise. Some countries return this tax when you leave.

- Always keep receipts for everything you buy!

SIGNS TO LOOK FOR:

ALMACEN (DEPARTMENT STORE)

BAZAR (DEPARTMENT STORE, SPAIN)

LIBRERIA (BOOK STORE)

PANADERIA (BAKERY)

MERCADO (MARKET)

SUPERMERCADO (SUPERMARKET)

KEY WORDS

Credit card

La tarjeta de crédito

L@ T@R-H@´-T@ D@
KR@´-D@-T@

Money

El dinero

@L D@-N@´-R@

Receipt

El recibo

@L R@-S@´-B@

Sale

La venta

L@ V@´N-T@

Store

La tienda

L@ T@-@´N-D@

Travelers' check

El cheque de viajero

@L CH@´-K@ D@
V@-@-H@´-R@

USEFUL PHRASES

Do you sell...?

¿Vende usted...?

VĕN-DA ⓞⓞS-TĕD...

Do you have...?

¿Tiene usted...?

TEE-ĕ-NA ⓞⓞS-TĕD...

I want to buy...

Quisiera comprar...

KEE-SEE-ĕ-Rah KOM-PRahR...

How much?

¿Cuánto es?

KWahN-TO ĕS

When are the shops open?

¿Cuándo se abren las tiendas?

KWahN-DO SA ah-BRĕN LahS TEE-ĕN-DahS

No thank you

No, gracias

NO GRah-SEE-ahS

I´m just looking

Estoy solo mirando

ĕS-T⊚ý S⊙́-L⊙ MⒺE-Ⓡah́N-D⊙

It's very expensive

!Es muy caro!

ĕS MWⒺE Kah́-Ⓡ⊙

Can't you give me a discount?

¿No me da una rebaja?

N⊙ MⒶ Dah ⊚o-Nah ⓇⒶ-Bah́-Hah

I'll take it!

¡Me lo llevo!

MⒶ L⊙ YⒶ́-V⊙

I'd like a receipt please

Quiero un recibo por favor

KⒺE-ĕ́-Ⓡ⊙ ⊚oN ⓇⒶ-SⒺE-B⊙ PFV

I want to return this

Quiero devolver esto

KⒺE-ĕ́-Ⓡ⊙ DⒶ-V⊙L-VĕR ĕS-T⊙

It doesn't fit

No me viene

N⊙ MⒶ V①-ĕ́-NⒶ

PHRASEMAKER

I'm looking for...

Busco...

B⬤⬤´S-K⬤...

---

a bakery

una panadería

⬤⬤-N⬤   P⬤-N⬤-D⬤-R⬤´-⬤

---

a bank

un banco

⬤⬤N   B⬤´N-K⬤

---

a barber shop

una peluquería

⬤⬤-N⬤   P⬤-L⬤-K⬤-R⬤´-⬤

---

a book store

una librería

⬤⬤-N⬤   L⬤-BR⬤-R⬤´-⬤

---

a camera shop

una tienda de fotografía

⬤⬤N-⬤   T⬤-⬤´N-D⬤   D⬤
F⬤-T⬤-GR⬤-F⬤´-⬤

a florist shop

una florería

ⓄⓄ́-Nⓐ FLⓄ-Rⓔ̃-Rⓔⓔ-ⓐ

a hair salon

una salon de belleza

ⓄⓄ́-Nⓐ Sⓐ-Lⓐ́N DⒶ BⒶ-YⒶ́-Sⓐ

a pharmacy

una farmacia

ⓄⓄ́-Nⓐ Fⓐ̃R-Mⓐ́-Sⓔⓔ-ⓐ

Do you sell...

Vende usted...

Vⓔ̃N-DⒶ ⓄⓄS-Tⓔ̃D...

aspirin?

aspirina?

ⓐ-SPⒺⒺ-Rⓔⓔ́-Nⓐ

cigarettes?

cigarrillos?

SⒺⒺ-Gⓐ-Rⓔⓔ́-YⓄS

clothes?	dresses?	shirts?
ropa?	vestidos?	camisas?
RⓄ́-Pⓐ	Vⓔ̃-STⒺⒺ́-DⓄS	Kⓐ-MⒺⒺ́-Sⓐ̃S

deodorant?

desodorante?

DⒶ-SⓄ-DⓄ-RⓐⓗN-TⒶ

film?

rollo de cámara?

RⓄ́-YⓄ   DⒶ   Kⓐⓗ-Mⓐⓗ-Rⓐⓗ

pantyhose?

pantimedias?

PⓐⓗN-TⒺⒺ-MⒶ́-DⒺⒺ-ⓐⓗS

perfume?

perfume?

PⒺ̃R-FⓄⓄ́-MⒶ

razor blades?

hojas de afeitar?

Ⓞ́-HⓐⓗS   DⒶ   ⓐⓗ-FⒶ-Tⓐⓗ́R

shaving cream?

crema de afeitar?

KRⒶ́-Mⓐⓗ   DⒶ   ⓐⓗ-FⒶ-Tⓐⓗ́R

soap?   **shampoo?**

jabón?   champú?

Hⓐⓗ-BⓄ́N   CHⓐⓗM-PⓄⓄ́

sunglasses?

anteojos para el sol?

@N-T@-O'-H@S P@-R@ @L S@L

sunscreen?

aceite para broncear?

@-S@'-T@ P@-R@

BR@N-S@-@'R

toothbrushes?

cepillos de dientes?

S@-P@'-Y@S D@ D@-@'N-T@S

toothpaste?

pasta de dientes?

P@'S-T@ D@ D@-@'N-T@S

water? (purified)

agua purificada?

@'-GW@ P@-R@-F@-C@-D@

water? (mineral)

agua mineral?

@'-GW@ M@-N@-R@L

ESSENTIAL SERVICES

Placing phone calls, mailing postcards and exchanging money are a few tasks you may need to perform while traveling.

THE BANK

As a traveler your primary contact with banks will be to exchange money.

- Have your passport handy when changing money.

- Change enough funds before leaving home to pay for tips, food and transportation to your final destination.

- Generally, you will receive a better rate of exchange at a a bank than at an exchange office or airport.

- Current exchange rates are posted in banks and published daily in city newspapers.

SIGNS TO LOOK FOR:

BANCO (BANK)

CASA DE CAMBIO (EXCHANGE OFFICE)

KEY WORDS

Bank

El banco

ⓔL BⓐⓗN-Kⓞ

Exchange office

La casa de cambio

Lⓐⓗ Kⓐⓗ-Sⓐⓗ Dⓐ KⓐⓗM-Bⓔⓔ-ⓞ

Money

El dinero

ⓔL Dⓔⓔ-Nⓐ-Rⓞ

Money order

El giro postal

ⓔL Hⓔⓔ-Rⓞ Pⓞs-TⓐⓗL

Travelers' check

El cheque de viajero

ⓔL CHⓐ-Kⓐ Dⓐ Vⓔⓔ-ⓐⓗ-Hⓐ-Rⓞ

Currencies

Peso/Mexico	Sol/Perú	Peseta/Spain
Pⓐ-Sⓞ	Sⓞl	Pⓐ-Sⓐ-Tⓐⓗ
Balboa/Panama	Colón/Salvador	Peso/Chile
BⓐⓗL-Bⓞ-ⓐⓗ	Kⓞ-LⓞN	Pⓐ-Sⓞ

USEFUL PHRASES

Where is the bank?

¿Dónde está el banco?

DÓN-DA ĕS-Táh ĕL BaͪN-KO

What time does the bank open?

¿A qué hora se abre el banco?

aͪ KA O-Raͪ SA aͪ-BRA
ĕL BaͪN-KO

Where is the Exchange Office?

¿Dónde está la casa de cambio?

DÓN-DA ĕS-Táh Laͪ Káh-Saͪ
DA KaͪM-BEE-O

What time does the Exchange Office open?

¿A qué hora se abre la casa de cambio?

aͪ KA O-Raͪ SA aͪ-BRĕ Laͪ
Káh-Saͪ DA KaͪM-BEE-O

Can I change dollars here?

¿Puedo cambiar dólares aquí?

PWÁ-DO KaͪM-BEE-aͪR
DÓ-Laͪ-RĕS aͪ-KEE

Can you change this?

¿Me puede cambiar esto?

Mⓐ PWⓐ́-Dⓐ KⓐʰM-BⓔⒺ-ⓐʰR
ⓔ̈S-Tⓞ

What is the exchange rate?

¿A cuánto está el cambio?

ⓐʰ KWⓐʰ́N-Tⓞ ⓔ̈S-Tⓐʰ́
ⓔ̈L Kⓐʰ́M-BⓔⒺ-ⓞ

I would like large bills

Quisiera billetes grandes

KⒺⒺ-SⒺⒺ-ⓔ̈́-Rⓐʰ BⒺⒺ-Yⓔ̈́-Tⓐved S
GRⓐʰ́N-Dⓔ̈S

I would like small bills

Quisiera billetes pequeños

KⒺⒺ-SⒺⒺ-ⓔ̈́-Rⓐʰ BⒺⒺ-Yⓔ̈́-Tⓐved S
Pⓐ-Kⓐ́N-Yⓞ S

I need change

Necesito cambio

Nⓐ-Sⓐ-SⒺⒺ́-Tⓞ Kⓐʰ́M-BⓔⒺ-ⓞ

POST OFFICE

If you are planning to send letters and postcards, be sure to send them early so that you don't arrive home before they do. **Correro** identifies the post office.

KEY WORDS

Air mail

Por avión

POR ah-VEE-ON

Letter

La carta

Lah KahR-Tah

Post office

El correo

eL KO-BA-O

Postcard

La tarjeta postal

Lah TahR-HA-Tah POS-TahL

Stamp

El sello

eL SA-YO

USEFUL PHRASES

Where is the post office?

¿Dónde está el correo?

DŌN-DA̧ ĕS-Ta̧h ĕL KO-B̧A̧-O

What time does the post office open?

¿A qué hora se abren los correos?

a̧h KA Ó-B̧a̧h SA a̧hB-B̧ĕN
LOS KO-B̧A̧-OS

I need...

Necesito...

↓ NA-SA-SĒ-TO...

stamps

unos sellos

ōō-NOS SA̧-YOS

an envelope

un sobre

ōōN SŌ-B̧B̧A

a pen

una pluma

ōō-Na̧h PLōō-Ma̧h

TELEPHONE

Placing phone calls in a foreign country can be a test of will and stamina! Besides the obvious language barriers, the quality of service can vary greatly from one city to the next.

- If you have a choice, do not call from your hotel room. Service charges can add a hefty amount to your bill.

- In Spain try to get to the CENTRAL TELEFONICA (CTNE). Here you can get assistance placing your call. You pay as soon as the call is completed.

- In Mexico, phone calls can be made from the post office.

SIGNS TO LOOK FOR:

CABINAS TELEFONICAS (PUBLIC TELEPHONES)

TELEFONOS (TELEPHONES)

KEY WORDS

Information

Información

EEN-FOR-Mah-SEE-ON

Long distance

Larga distancia

Lah'R-Gah DEES-Tah'N-SEE-ah

Operator

La operadora

Lah O-PA-Rah-DOR-ah

Phone book

La guía telefónica

Lah GEE-ah TA-LA-FO-NEE-Kah

Public telephone

Teléfono público

TA-LA-FO-NO POOB-LEE-KO

Telephone

El teléfono

EL TA-LA-FO-NO

USEFUL PHRASES

May I use your telephone?

¿Puedo usar su teléfono?

PWA-DO oo-SahB Soo
TA-LA-FO-NO

Operator, I don't speak Spanish

Operadora, no hablo español

O-PA-Bah-DOB-ah NO ahB-LO
eS-PahN-YOL

I want to call this number:

Quiero marcar este numero:

KEE-e-BO MahB-KahB
eS-TA Noo-MA-BO

1 uno oo-NO		**2** dos DOS	
3 tres TBAS		**4** cuatro KWah-TBO	
5 cinco SEEN-KO		**6** seis SAS	
7 siete SEE-e-TA		**8** ocho O-CHO	
9 nueve NWe-VA		**0** cero SA-BO	

PHRASEMAKER

I would like to make a call...

Quisiera hacer una llamada...

K(EE)-S(EE)-(e)́-R(ah) (ah)-S(e)́R
(oo)́-N(ah) Y(ah)-M(ah)́-D(ah)...

long distance

de larga distancia

D(A) L(ah)́R-G(ah) D(EE)S-T(ah)́N-S(EE)-(ah)

collect

por cobrar

P(O)R K(O)-BR(ah)́R

person to person

persona a persona

P(e)́R-S(O)́-N(ah) (ah) P(e)́R-S(O)́-N(ah)

to the United States

a los Estados Unidos

(ah) L(O)S (e)́S-T(ah)́-D(O)S
(oo)-N(EE)́-D(O)S

SIGHTSEEING
AND
ENTERTAINMENT

In most cities and towns in Spanish speaking countries, you will find tourist information offices. Here you can usually obtain brochures, maps, historical information, and bus and train schedules.

CITIES IN MEXICO

Ciudad de Mexico
SEE-oo-DahD DA MA-HEE-KO

Teotiuacan (ruins)
TA-O-TEE-oo-Wah-KahN

Acapulco
ah-Kah-PooL-KO

Cancun
KahN-KooN

CITIES IN SOUTH AMERICA

Buenos Aires
BWA-NOS I-RAS

Santiago
SahN-TEE-ah-GO

Bogota
BO-Gah-Tah

Lima
LEE-Mah

CITIES IN SPAIN

Madrid
Mah-DREED

Barcelona
BahR-THE-LO-Nah

Sevilla (Seville)
SA-VEE-Yah

Pamplona
PahM-PLO-Nah

KEY WORDS

Admission

La admisión

L@ @D-M@-S@-O'N

Map

El mapa

@L M@-P@

Reservation

La reservación

L@ R@-S@R-V@-S@-O'N

Ticket

El boleto   El billete

@L B@-L@-T@   @L B@-Y@-T@

Tour

La excursión

L@ @KS-K@R-S@-O'N

Tour guide

El guía turística

@L G@-@ T@-R@S-T@-K@

USEFUL PHRASES

Where is the tourist office?

¿Dónde está la oficina de turismo?

DŌN-DĀ ĕS-Táh Láh

Ō-FĒE-SĒE-Náh DĀ TOO-RĒEZ-MŌ

Is there a tour to...?

¿Hay una excursión a...?

Ī OO-Náh ĕKS-KOOR-SĒE-ŌN áh...

Where do I buy a ticket?

¿Dónde compro la entrada?

DŌN-DĀ KŌM-PRŌ

Láh ĕN-TRáh-Dáh

How much does the tour cost?

¿Cuánto cuesta la excursión?

KWáhN-TŌ KWĕS-Táh

Láh ĕKS-KOOR-SĒE-ŌN

How long does the tour take?

¿Cuánto dura la excursión?

KWáhN-TŌ DOO-Ráh

Láh ĕKS-KOOR-SĒE-ŌN

Does the guide speak English?

¿Habla inglés el guia?

ah-BLah EEN-GLAS el GEE-ah

How much do children pay?

¿Cuánto pagan los niños?

KWahN-TO Pah-GahN LOS
NEEN-YOS

What time does the show start?

¿A qué hora empieza la función?

ah KA O-Rah eM-PEE-A-Sah
Lah FooN-SEE-ON

Do I need reservations?

¿Necesito una reserva?

NA-SA-SEE-TO oo-Nah
RA-SeR-Vah

Where can we go dancing?

¿Dónde está la disco?

DON-DA eS-Tah Lah DEES-KO

Is there a minimum cover charge?

¿Hay un cargo mínimo?

I ooN KahR-GO MEE-NEE-MO

PHRASEMAKER

May I invite you...

¿Puedo invitarle...

↓ PW(A)́-D(O) (EE)N-V(EE)-T(ah)́R-L(A)...

to a concert?

a un concierto?

(ah) (oo)N K(O)N-S(EE)-(ĕ)́R-T(O)

to dance?

a bailar?

(ah) B(I)-L(ah)́R

to dinner?

a cenar?

(ah) S(A)-N(ah)́R

to the movies?

al cine?

(ah)L S(EE)́-N(A)

to the theater?

al teatro?

(ah)L T(A)-(ah)́-TR(O)

Where can I find...

¿Dónde se encuentra...

DOON-DA SA ĕN-KWAN-TRah...

a golf course?

un campo de golf?

ooN KahM-PO DA GOLF

a health club?

un gimnasio?

ooN HEEM-Nah-SEE-O

a swimming pool?

una piscina?

oo-Nah PEE-SEE-Nah

a tennis court?

una cancha de tenís?

oo-Nah KahN-CHah
DA TA-NEES

HEALTH

Hopefully you will not need medical attention on your trip. If you do, it is important to communicate basic information regarding your condition.

- Check with your insurance company before leaving home to find out if you are covered in a foreign country.

- Have your prescriptions translated before you leave home.

- Take a small first aid kit with you on your trip. Include Band Aids, aspirin, cough syrup, throat lozenges, and vitamins.

- Your Embassy or Consulate should be able to assist you in finding health care.

SIGNS TO LOOK FOR:

Ⓗ (HOSPITAL)

HOSPITAL

CASA DE SOCCORO (EMERGENCY FIRST AID CENTER)

CRUZ ROJA (RED CROSS)

KEY WORDS

Ambulance

La ambulancia

Lah ahM-Boo-LahN-SEE-ah

Dentist

El dentista

êL DêN-TEE'S-Tah

Doctor

El médico

êL MA'-DEE-KO

Emergency

La emergencia

Lah A-MêR-HêN-SEE-ah

Hospital

El hospital

êL OS-PEE-Tah'L

Prescription

La receta

Lah RA-SA'-Tah

USEFUL PHRASES

I am sick

Estoy enfermo (male)
Estoy enferma (female)

ĕS-Tŏý ĕN-FĔR-MŎ

ĕS-Tŏý ĕN-FĔR-Mah

I need a doctor

Necesito ayuda

NⒶ-SⒶ-SEÉ-TŎ ah-Yoó-Dah

It's an emergency!

¡Es una emergencia!

ĕS oó-Nah Ⓐ-MĔR-HĔN-SEE-ah

Where is the nearest hospital?

¿Dónde está el hospital más cerca?

DŎ́N-DⒶ ĕS-Tah́ ĕL

ŎS-PEE-Tah́L Mah S SĔR-Kah

Call an ambulance!

Lláme una ambulancia!

Yah́-MⒶ oó-Nah

ah M-Boo-Lah́N-SEE-ah PFV

I'm allergic to...

Tengo alergias a...

TⓔN-GⓄ ⓐ-LⓔR-HⒺ-ⓐS ⓐ...

I'm pregnant

Estoy embarazada

ⓔS-Tⓞⓨ ⓔM-Bⓐ-Rⓐ-Sⓐ-Dⓐ

I'm diabetic

Soy diabético (male)
Soy diabética (female)

Sⓞⓨ DⒺ-ⓐ-BⒶ-TⒺ-KⓄ

Sⓞⓨ DⒺ-ⓐ-BⒶ-TⒺ-Kⓐ

I have a heart condition

Sufro del corazón

Sⓞⓞ-FRⓄ DⓔL KⓄ-Rⓐ-SⓄN

I have high/ low blood pressure

Tengo la tensión alta/baja

TⓔN-GⓄ Lⓐ TⓔN-SⒺ-ⓄN

ⓐL-Tⓐ / Bⓐ-Hⓐ

high / low

PHRASEMAKER

I need...

Necesito...

N(A)-S(A)-S(EE)-T(O)...

a doctor

a un médico

(ah)   (oo)N   M(A)-D(EE)-K(O)

a dentist

a un dentista

(ah)   (oo)N   D(e)N-T(EE)S-T(ah)

a nurse

a una enfermera

(ah)   (oo)-N(ah)   (e)N-F(e)R-M(A)-R(ah)

an optician

un óptico

(oo)N   (O)P-T(EE)-C(O)

a pharmacist

un farmacéutico

(oo)N   F(ah)R-M(ah)-S(oo)-T(EE)-K(O)

(AT THE PHARMACY)

Do you have...

¿Tiene usted...

TEE-ê'-NA   ooS-TêD...

aspirin?

aspirina?

ahS-PEE-REE'-Nah

band aids?

curitas?

Koo-REE'-TahS

cough syrup?

calmante de la tos?

KahL-Mah'N-TA DA Lah TOS

ear drops?

gotas para los oídos?

GO'-TahS Pah'-Rah
LOS O-EE'-DOS

eye drops?

gotas para los ojos?

GO'-TahS Pah'-Rah LOS O'-HOS

PHRASES FOR BUSINESS TRAVELERS

This section provides some basic words and phrases for the business person in a Spanish speaking country. It is important to show appreciation and interest in another person's language and culture. A few well pronounced phrases can make a great impression.

KEY WORDS

Appointment
La cita

L(ah) S(EE)́-T(ah)

Meeting
La reunión

L(ah) R(A)-(oo)N-Y(O)́N

Marketing
El mercado técnico

(e)L M(e)R-K(ah)́-D(O) T(e)́K-N(EE)-K(O)

Presentation
La presentación

L(ah) PR(e)-S(e)N-T(ah)-S(EE)-(O)́N

Sales
Las ventas

L(ah)S V(e)́N-T(ah)S

USEFUL PHRASES

I have an appointment

Tengo una cita

TĒN-GO͞ o͞o-Nah SĒE-Tah

I want to make an appointment with...

Quisiera hacer una cita con...

KĒE-SĒE-ē-Rah ah-SĒR o͞o-Nah SĒE-Tah KON...

Here is my card

Aquí tiene mi tarjeta personal

ah-KĒE TĒE-ē-NA MĒE Tah-R-HA-Tah PĒR-SO-Nah-L

Can we get an interpreter?

¿Hay un interprete?

I͞ o͞oN ĒEN-TĒR-PRA-TA

May I speak to Mr...?

¿Se encuentra el señor...?

SA ĒN-KWA-N-TRah ēL SA-N-YOR...

May I speak to Mrs...?

¿Se encuentra la señora...?

SA ĒN-KWA-N-TRah Lah SA-N-YO-Rah...

PHRASEMAKER

I need...

Necesito...

↓ N(A)-S(A)-S(EE)-T(O)...

---

a computer

una computadora
un ordenador (Spain)

(OO)-N(ah) K(O)M-P(oo)-T(ah)-D(O)-R(ah)

(OO)N (O)R-D(A)-N(ah)-D(O)R

---

a copy machine

una máquina para hacer copias

(OO)-N(ah) M(ah)-K(EE)-N(ah) P(ah)-R(ah)

(ah)-S(ê)R K(O)-P(EE)-(ah)S

---

a conference room

un salón de conferencia

(OO)N S(ah)-L(O)N D(A)

K(O)N-F(A)-R(ê)N-S(EE)-(ah)

---

a fax or a fax machine

un fax

(OO)N F(ah)KS

↓

an interpreter

un intérprete

ⓞⓞN ⓔⓔN-Tⓔ́R-PRⒶ-TⒶ

a lawyer

un abogado

ⓞⓞN Ⓐ-BⓄ-GⒶ́-DⓄ

a notary

un notario

ⓞⓞN NⓄ-TⒶ́-RⒺⒺ-Ⓞ

overnight delivery

entrega expresa
entrega enmediata (Spain)

Ⓔ́N-TRⒶ́-GⒶ ⒺKS-PRⒺ́-SⒶ

Ⓔ́N-TRⒶ́-GⒶ ⒺN-MⒶ-DⒺⒺ-Ⓐ́-TⒶ

paper

papel

PⒶ-PⒺ́L

a secretary

una secretaria

ⓞⓞ́-NⒶ SⒺ́-KRⒶ-TⒶ́-RⒺⒺ-Ⓐ

GENERAL INFORMATION

THE DAYS

Monday
lunes
LOO-NĕS

Tuesday
martes
Mah̄R-TĕS

Wednesday
miércoles
MEE-ĕ̄R-KO-LĕS

Thursday
jueves
HWÁ-VĕS

Friday
viernes
VEE-ĕ̄R-NĕS

Saturday
sábado
Sah́-Bah-DO

Sunday
domingo
DO-MEéN-GO

THE MONTHS

January
enero
Á-NÁ-RO

February
febrero
FÁ-BRÁ-RO

March
marzo
Mah̄R-SO

April
abril
ah-BREéL

May
mayo

Mâh-YO

June
junio

Hoo-NEE-O

July
julio

Hoo-LEE-O

August
agosto

âh-GOS-TO

September
septiembre

SêP-TEE-êM-BRA

October
octubre

OK-Too-BRA

November
noviembre

NO-VEE-êM-BRA

December
diciembre

DEE-SEE-êM-BRA

Spring
La primavera

Lâh PREE-Mâh-VA-Bâh

Summer
El verano

êL Vê-Bâh-NO

Autumn
El otoño

êL O-TON-YO

Winter
El invierno

êL

EEN-VEE-êR-NO

NUMBERS

0	1	2
Cero	Uno	Dos
SĀ-RO	OO-NO	DOS

3	4	5
Tres	Cuatro	Cinco
TRĀS	KWah-TRO	SEEN-KO

6	7	8
Seis	Siete	Ocho
SĀS	SEE-ĕ-TĀ	O-CHO

9	10	11
Nueve	Diez	Once
NWĀ-VĀ	DEE-ĕS	ON-SĀ

12	13	14
Doce	Trece	Catorce
DO-SĀ	TRĀ-SĀ	Kah-TOR-SĀ

15	16
Quince	Dieciséis
KEEN-SĀ	DEE-ĕS-EE-SĀS

17

Diecisiete

DEE-ĕS-EE-SEE-ĕ-TĀ

18
Dieciocho

DEE-ĕS-EE-Ó-CHO

19
Diecinueve

DEE-ĕS-EE-NWÁ-VA

20	30
Veinte	Treinta
VÁN-TA	TRÁN-Tah

40	50
Cuarenta	Cincuenta
KWah-RÁN-Tah	SEEN-KWÁN-Tah

100	1000
Cien	Mil
SEE-ĕN	MEEL

1,000,000
Millón

MEE-YÓN

COLORS

Black

Negro

NA´-GRO

Blue

Azul

ah-SOOL

Brown

Café

Kah-FA´

Gold

Oro

O´-RO

Gray

Grís

GREES

Green

Verde

VeR-DA

Orange

Anaranjado

ah-N-ah-R-ah-N-H-ah-DO

Pink

Rosado

RO-S-ah-DO

Purple

Morado

MO-R-ah-DO

Red

Rojo

RO-HO

White

Blanco

BL-ah-N-KO

Yellow

Amarillo

ah-M-ah-R-EE-YO

DICTIONARY

Gender of nouns is indicated by **(m)** for masculine and **(f)** for feminine. Plural is indicated by **(/pl)**. Adjectives are shown in their masculine form, as common practice dictates. Adjectives and some nouns that end in **o** or **os** can usually be changed to feminine by changing the ending to **a** or **as**. Verbs appear in the first person singular.

Each English entry is followed by the Spanish spelling and the EPLS spelling.

A

a,an un (m), una (f) ooN oo-Nah
a lot mucho Moo-CHO
able (to be) poder PO-DeR
above sobre SO-BRA
accident accidente (m) ahK-SEE-DeN-TA
accommodation alojamiento (m)
  ah-LO-Hah-MEE-eN-TO
account cuenta (f) KWeN-Tah
address dirección (f) DEE-ReK-SEE-ON
admission admisión (f) ahD-MEE-SEE-ON
afraid tener miedo TeN-eR MEE-A-DO
after después DeS-PWAS
afternoon tarde (f) TahR-DA
agency agencia (f) ah-HeN-SEE-Yah
air-conditioning aire acondicionado (m)
  Ī-RA ah-KON-DEE-SEE-O-Nah-DO
aircraft avión (m) ah-VEE-ON
airline línea aérea (f) LEE-NA-ah ah-Ī-RA-ah
airport aeropuerto (m) Ī-RO-PWeR-TO
aisle pasillo (m) Pah-SEE-YO
all todo TO-DO

almost casi   KAH-SEE

alone solo   SO-LO

also también   TAHM-BEE-eN

always siempre   SEE-eM-PRAH

ambulance ambulancia (f)   AHM-Boo-LAHN-SEE-ah

American americano (m)   ah-ME-REE-KAH-NO

and y   EE

another otro   O-TRO

anything algo   AHL-GO

apartment apartamento (m)   ah-PAHR-TAH-MeN-TO

appetizers entremeses (m/pl)   eN-TRAH-MAH-SeS

apple manzana (f)   MAHN-SAH-NAH

appointment cita (f)   SEE-TAH

April abril (m)   ah-BReeL

arrival llegada (f)   YA-GAH-DAH

arrive (to) llegar   YA-GAHR

ashtray cenicero (m)   Se-NEE-SA-RO

aspirin aspirina (f)   ah-SPEE-REE-NAH

attention ¡atención!   ah-TeN-SEE-ON

August agosto (m)   ah-GOS-TO

author autor (m)   OW-TOR

automobile automóvil (m)   OW-TO-MO-VeL

Autumn otoño (m)   O-TON-YO

avenue avenida (f)   ah-VeN-EE-DAH

awful horrible   O-ReE-BLAH

B

baby bebé (m)   BA-BA

babysitter niñera (f)   NEEN-YA-RAH

bacon tocino (m)   TO-SEE-NO

bad malo   MAH-LO

bag maleta (f)   MAH-LA-TAH

baggage equipaje (m)   A-KEE-Pah-HA

baked al horno   ahL OR-NO

bakery panadería (f)   Pah-Nah-DA-REE-ah

banana plátano (m)   PLah-Tah-NO

band aid curita (f)   Koo-REE-Tah

bank banco (m)   BahN-KO

barber shop peluquería (f)   PA-Loo-KA-REE-ah

bartender cantinero (m)   KahN-TEE-NA-RO

bath baño (m)   BahN-YO

bathing suit traje de baño (m)   TRah-HA DA BahN-YO

bathroom baño (m)   BahN-YO

battery batería (f), pila (f)   Bah-TA-REE-ah, PEE-Lah

beach playa (f)   PLah-Yah

beautiful bello   BA-YO

beauty shop salón de belleza (f)
    Sah-LON DA BA-YA-Sah

bed cama (f)   Kah-Mah

beef carne de res (f)   KahB-NA DA RES

beer cerveza (f)   SeB-VA-Sah

bellman botones (m)   BO-TO-NeS

belt cinturón (m)   SEEN-Too-RON

big grande   GRahN-DA

bill cuenta (f)   KWeN-Tah

black negro   NA-GRO

blanket cobija (f), KO-BEE-Hah
    manta (f) (Spain)   MahN-Tah

blue azul   ah-SooL

boat barco (m)   BahB-KO

book libro (m)   LEE-BRO

book store librería (f)   LEE-BRA-REE-ah

border frontera (f)   FRON-TA-Bah

boy muchacho (m) Moo-CHah-CHO

bracelet pulsera (f) Pool-SA-Bah

brake freno (m) FBA-NO

bread pan (m) Pahn

breakfast desayuno (m) Dé-Sah-Yoo-NO

broiled a la parrilla ah Lah Pah-Bee-ah

brown café Kah-FA

brush cepillo (m) SA-Pee-YO

building edificio (m) A-Dee-Fee-See-O

bus autobús (m) ow-TO-Boo's

bus station estación de autobúses (f) é-STah-See-O'N
   DA ow-TO-Boo'-Sés

bus stop parada de autobúses (f)
   Pah-Bah-Dah DA ow-TO-Boo's

business negocios (m) NA-GO-See-OS

butter mantequilla (f) Mahn-TA-Kee-Yah

buy (to) comprar KOM-PBahB

C

cab taxi (m) Tah'K-See

call (to) llamar Yah-MahB

call llamada (f) Yah-Mah-Dah

camera cámara (f) Kah-Mah-Bah

candy dulce (m) Doo-L-SA

car carro (m), coche m) automóvil (m)
   Kah-BO, KO-CHA, ow-TO-MO-VeeL

carrot zanahoria (f) Sah-NO-Bee-ah

castle castillo (m) Kah-STee-YO

cathedral catedral (f) Kah-TA-DBahL

celebration celebración (f) SA-LA-BBah-See-O'N

center centro Sé'N-TBO

cereal cereal (m) SA-BA-ahL

chair silla (f) SEE-Yah

champagne champaña (f) CHahM-PahN-Yah

change, exact cambio exacto (m)
    KahM-BEE-O EK-SahK-TO

change (money) cambio (m) KahM-BEE-O

change (to) cambiar KahM-BEE-ahR

cheap barato Bah-Rah-TO

check (restaurant bill) cuenta (f) KWEN-Tah

cheers! ¡salud! Sah-LooD

cheese queso (m) KA-SO

chicken pollo (m) PO-YO

child niño (m), niña (f) NEEN-YO, NEEN-Yah

chocolate chocolate CHO-KO-Lah-TA

church iglesia (f) EE-GLA-SEE-ah

cigar cigarro (m), puro (m) SEE-Gah-RO, Poo-RO

cigarette cigarrillo (m) SEE-Gah-REE-YO

city ciudad (f) SEE-oo-DahD

clean limpio LEEM-PEE-O

close (to) cerrar SA-RahR

closed cerrado SE-Rah-DO

clothes ropa (f) RO-Pah

cocktail coctél (m) KOK-TEL

coffee café (m) Kah-FA

cold frío FREE-O

comb peine (m) PA-NA

come (to) venir VE-NEER

company compañía (f) KOM-PahN-YEE-ah

computer computadora (f) KOM-Poo-Tah-DO-Rah
    ordenador (m) (Spain) OR-DA-Nah-DOR

concert concierto (m) KON-SEE-ER-TO

conference conferencia (f) KON-FA-REN-SEE-ah

conference room salón de conferencia (m)
Sah-LON DA KON-Fah-Ren-See-ah

congratulations felicitaciones (f)
FA-Lee-See-Tah-See-O-NeS

copy machine máquina para hacer copias (f)
Mah-Kee-Nah Pah-Rah ah-SeR KO-Pee-ahS
xerox (m) Zee-RahKS

corn maíz (m) Mah-eeS

cough syrup calmante de la tos (m)
KahL-Mah'N-TA DA Lah TOS

cover charge cargo mínimo (m) Kah'R-GO Mee-Nee-MO

crab cangrejo (m) Kah'N-GRA-HO

cream crema (f) KRA-Mah

credit card tarjeta de crédito (f)
Tah'R-HA-Tah DA KRA-Dee-TO

cup taza (f) Tah-Sah

customs aduana (f) ah-DWah-Nah

D

dance (to) bailar Bi-Lah'R

dangerous peligroso Pe-Lee-GRO-SO

date (calender) fecha (f) FA-CHah

day día (m) Dee-ah

December diciembre (m) Dee-See-eM-BRah

delicious delicioso DA-Lee-See-O-SO

delighted encantado eN-Kah'N-Tah-DO

dentist dentista (m) DeN-Tees-Tah

deodorant desodorante (m) DA-SO-DO-Rah'N-TA

department store almacén (m) ahL-Mah-SeN

departure salida (f) Sah-Lee-Dah

dessert postre (m) POS-TRah

detour desviación (f) DeS-Vee-ah-See-ON

diabetic diabético (m) Dee-ah-BA-Te-KO

diarrhea diarrea (f) Dee-ah-RA-ah

dictionary diccionario (m) Deek-See-O-Nah-Ree-O

dinner cena (f) SA-Nah

dining room comedor (m) KO-MA-DOR

direction dirección (f) Dee-Rek-See-ON

dirty sucio Soo-See-O

disabled inválidos een-Vah-Lee-DOS

discount descuento (m) DeS-KWeN-TO
      rebaja (f) RA-Bah-Hah

distance distancia (f) DeeS-Tahn-See-ah

doctor médico (m) MA-Dee-KO

document documento (m) DO-Koo-MeN-TO

dollar dólar (m) DO-Lahr

down abajo ah-Bah-HO

downtown el centro eL SeN-TRO

dress vestido (m) VeS-Tee-DO

drink (to) beber BA-BeR, tomar TO-Mahr

drive (to) manejar Mah-NA-Hahr

drugstore farmácia (f) Fahr-Mah-See-ah

dry cleaner tintorería (f) TeeN-TO-RA-Ree-ah

duck pato (m) Pah-TO

E

ear oreja (f), inner ear oído (m) O-RA-Hah, O-EE-DO

ear drops gotas para los oídos (f/pl)
      GO-Tahs Pah-Rah LOS O-EE-DOS

early temprano TeM-PRah-NO

east este (m) eS-TA

easy fácil Fah-SeeL

eat (to) comer KO-MeR

egg huevo (m)   WA-VO

eggs, fried huevos fritos (m/pl)   WA-VOS FREE-TOS

eggs, scrambled huevos revueltos (m/pl)
  WA-VOS RA-VWEL-TOS

electricity electricidad (f)   A-LEK-TREE-SEE-DaD

elevator ascensor (m)   ah-SEN-SOR

embassy embajada (f)   EM-Bah-Hah-Dah

emergency emergencia (f)   A-MER-HEN-SEE-ah

English inglés (m)   EN-GLAS

enough! ¡Basta!   BahS-Tah

entrance entrada (f)   EN-TRah-Dah

envelope sobre (m)   SO-BRA

evening tarde (f)   TahR-DA

everything todo   TO-DO

excellent excelente   EK-SA-LEN-TA

excuse me perdón   PER-DON

exit salida (f)   Sah-LEE-Dah

expensive caro   Kah-RO

eye ojo (m)   O-HO

eye drops gotas para los ojos (f/pl)   GO-TahS Pah-Rah
  LOS O-HOS

F

face cara (f)   Kah-Rah

far lejos   LA-HOS

fare pasaje(m)   Pah-Sah-HA

fast rápido   Rah-PEE-DO

fax, fax machine fax (m)   FahKS

February febrero (m)   FA-BRA-RO

few poco   PO-KO

film (for a camera) rollo de cámara (m)
  RO-YO DA Kah-Mah-Rah

film (movie) película PⒶ-LⒺ̄-KⓄⓄ-Lⓐh

fine/ very well muy bien MWⒺ̄ BⒺ̄-Ⓔ̃N

finger dedo (m) DⒶ̄-DⓄ

fingernail uña (f) ⓄⓄN-Yⓐh

fire extinguisher extintor (m) Ⓔ̃KS-TⒺ̃N-TⓄR

fire fuego (m) FWⒶ̄-GⓄ

fire! ¡incendio! Ⓔ̄N-SⒺ̃N-DⒺ̄-Ⓞ

first primero PRⒺ̄-MⒶ̄-RⓄ

fish pescado (m) PⒺ̃S-Kⓐh-DⓄ

flight vuelo (m) VWⒶ̄-LⓄ

floor (story) piso (m) PⒺ̄-SⓄ

florist shop florería (f) FLⓄ-RⒺ̃-RⒺ̄-ⓐh

flower flor (f) FLⓄR

food comida (f) KⓄ-MⒺ̄-Dⓐh

foot pie (m) PⒺ̄-Ⓐ

fork tenedor (m) TⒺ̃-Nⓐh-DⓄR

french fries papas fritas (f/pl) Pⓐh-PⓐhS FRⒺ̄-TⓐhS
        patatas fritas (Spain) Pⓐh-Tⓐh-TⓐhS FRⒺ̄-TⓐhS

fresh fresco FRⒺ̃S-KⓄ

Friday viernes (m) VⒺ̄-Ⓔ̃R-NⒺ̃S

fried frito FRⒺ̄-TⓄ

friend amigo (m), amiga (f) ⓐh-MⒺ̄-GⓄ, ⓐh-MⒺ̄-Gⓐh

fruit fruta (f) FRⓄⓄ-Tⓐh

funny gracioso GRⓐh-SⒺ̄-Ⓞ-SⓄ

G

gas station gasolinera (f) Gⓐh-SⓄ-LⒺ̄-NⒶ̄-Rⓐh

gasoline petróleo (f) PⒶ̄-TRⓄ-LⒶ̄-Ⓞ

gate puerta (f) PWⒺ̃R-Tⓐh

gentleman caballero (m) Kⓐh-Bⓐh-YⒶ̄-RⓄ

gift regalo (m) RⒺ̃-Gⓐh-LⓄ

girl muchacha (f) MⓄⓄ-CHⓐh-CHⓐh

glass (drinking) vaso (m) VAH-SO

glasses (eye) lentes (m/pl) LEN-TES

glove guante (m) GWAHN-TA

go vaya VAH-YAH

gold oro (m) O-RO

golf golf (m) GOLF

golf course campo de golf (m) KAHM-PO DA GOLF

good bueno BWA-NO

goodbye adiós ahD-YOS

goose ganso (m) GAHN-SO

grape uva (f) OO-VAH

grateful agradecido ah-GRAH-DA-SEE-DO

gray grís GREES

green verde VER-DA

grocery store tienda de comestibles (f)
TEE-EN-DAH DA KO-MES-TEE-BLES

group grupo (m) GROO-PO

guide guía (m) GEE-ah

H

hair cabello (m) KAH-BA-YO

hairbrush cepillo (m) SA-PEE-YO

haircut corte de pelo (m) KOR-TA DA PA-LO

ham jamón HAH-MON

hamburger hamburguesa (f) ahM-BOOR-GA-SAH

hand la mano (f) LAH MAH-NO

happy feliz FA-LEES

have, I tengo TEN-GO

he él EL

head cabeza (f) KAH-BA-SAH

headache dolor de cabeza (m)
DO-LOR DA CAH-BA-SAH

health club gimnasio (m) HEEM-Nah'-SEE-O
   club (m)   KLooB

heart condition sufro del corazón (m)
   SooʻFRO DEL KO-Rah-SOʻN

heart corazón (m)   KO-Rah-SOʻN

heat calefacción   Kah-LA-Fah'K-SEE-OʻN

hello hola   Oʻ-Lah

help! ¡socorro!, ¡auxilio!   SO-KOʻ-RO, ahX-SEEʻ-LEE-O

here aquí   ah-KEE

holiday día feriado (m)   DEEʻ-ah FA-REE-ahʻ-DO

hospital hospital (m)   OS-PEE-Tahl

hot dog hot dog (m)   EL Hah T Dah G

hotel hotel (m)   O-TEL

hour hora (f)   Oʻ-Rah

how ¿cómo? KOʻ-MO

hurry (to) tener prisa   TE-NER PREEʻ-Sah

hurry ¡apúrese!   ah-Poo-RA-SA

I

I yo   YO

ice hielo (m)   YAʻ-LO

ice cream helado (m)   A-Lahʻ-DO
   nieve (f) (Mexico) NEE-Aʻ-VA

ice cubes cubitos de hielo (m/pl)   Koo-BEEʻ-TOS DA
   YAʻ-LO

ill enfermo   EN-FEʻRB-MO

important importante   EEM-POR-TahʻN-TA

indigestion indegestión (f)   ON-DEE-HEʻS-TEYOʻN

information información (f)   EEN-FOR-Mah-SEE-OʻN

inn posada (f)   PO-Sahʻ-Dah

interpreter intérprete (m)   EEN-TEʻR-PRA-TA

J

jacket chaqueta (f) CHah-KA-Tah

jam mermelada (f) MeR-Me-LA-Dah

January enero (m) A-NA-RO

jewelry joyas (f) Hoy-ahS

jewelry store joyería (f) Hoy-e-REE-ah

job trabajo (m) TRah-Bah-HO

juice jugo Hoo-GO

July julio (m) Hoo-LEE-O

June junio (m) Hoo-NEE-O

K

ketchup ketchup (m) Ke-CHooP

key llave (f) Yah-VA

kiss beso (m) BA-SO

knife cuchillo (m) Koo-CHEE-YO

know, I Yo sé YO SA

L

ladies' restroom servicios de señoras (m)
SeR-VEE-SEE-OS DA SAN-YO-RahS

lady dama (f) Dah-Mah

lamb cordero (m) KOR-DA-RO

language idioma (m) EE-DEE-O-Mah

large grande GRahN-DA

late tarde TahR-DA

laundry lavandería (f) Lah-VahN-DA-REE-ah

lawyer abogado (m) ah-BO-Gah-DO

left (direction) izquierdo EES-KEE-eR-DO

leg pierna (f) PEE-eR-Nah

lemon limón (m) LEE-MON

less menos MA-NOS

letter carta (f) Kah-Tah

lettuce lechuga (f) LA-CHOO-Gah

light luz LOOS

like como KO-MO

like, I me gusta MA GOOS-Tah

like, I would me gustaría MA GOOS-Tah-REE-Yah

lip labio (m) Lah-BEE-O

lipstick pintura de labios (f)
    PEEN-TOO-Rah DA Lah-BEE-OS

little (amount) poquito PO-KEE-TO

little (size) pequeño PA-KEN-YO

live (to) vivir VEE-VEER

lobster langosta (f) Lah-N-GOS-Tah

long largo Lah-R-GO

lost perdido PER-DEE-DO

love amor (m) ah-MOR

luck suerte (f) SWER-Tah

luggage equipaje (m) A-KEE-Pah-HA

lunch almuerzo (m) ahL-MWER-SO

M

maid camarera (f), criada (f)
    Kah-Mah-RA-Rah, KREE-ah-Dah

mail correo (m) KO-RA-O

makeup maquillaje (m) Mah-KEE-Yah-HA

man hombre (m) OM-BRA

manager gerente (m) HA-REN-TA

map mapa (m) Mah-Pah

March marzo (m) Mah-R-SO

market mercado (m) MER-Kah-DO

match (light) cerillo (m), fósforo (m)
    SE-REE-O, FOS-FO-RO

May mayo (m) Mah-YO

mayonnaise mayonesa (f) MAH-YO-NA'-SAH

meal comida (f) KO-MEE-DAH

meat carne (f) KAH'R-NA

mechanic mecánico (m) MA-KAH-NEE-KO

medicine medicina (f) MA-DEE-SEE-NAH

meeting reunión (f) RA-OO-NEE-O'N

mens' restroom servicios de señores (m)
SER-VEE-SEE-OS DA SAN-YO'-RES

menu menú (m) MA-NOO, carta (f) CAHR-TAH

message recado (m) RA-KAH-DO

milk leche (f) LA'-CHA

mineral water agua mineral (m) AH-GWAH MEE-NA-RAHL

minute minuto (m) MEE-NOO-TO

Miss señorita (f) SAN-YO-REE-TAH

mistake error (f) E-ROR

misunderstanding equivocación (f) A-KEE-VO-KAH-SEE-O'N

moment momento (m) MO-MEN-TO

Monday lunes (m) LOO-NES

money dinero (m) DEE-NA'-RO

month mes (m) MES

monument monumento (m) MO-NOO-MEN-TO

more más MAHS

morning mañana (f) MAHN-YAH'-NAH

mosque mezquita (f) MES-KEE'-TAH

mother madre (f) MAH'-DRA

mountain montaña (f) MON-TAH'N-YAH

movies cine (m) SEE-NA

Mr. señor (m) SAN-YOR

Mrs. señora (f) SAN-YO'-RAH

much, too demaciado DEE-MAH-SEE-AH'-DO

museum museo (m) MOO-SA'-O

mushroom hongo (m)

music música (f) MOO'-SEE-KAH

mustard mostaza (f) MOS-TAH-SAH

N

nail polish esmalte para uñas (m)
  ES-MAHL-TA PAH-BAH OON-YAHS

name nombre (m) NOM-BBA

name (to) llamar (f) YAH-MAHB

napkin servilleta (f) SEB-VEE-YA-TAH

napkins (sanitary) toallitas (f) TO-AH-YEE-TAHS
  almohadillas higiénicas (f)
  AH-MO-HAH-DEE-YAHS EE-HEE-E-NEE-KAHS
  toallitas sanitarias (f) TO-AH-YEE-TAHS
  SAH-NE-TA-REE-AHS

near cerca SEB-KAH

neck cuello (m) KWA-YO

need, I necesito NA-SA-SEE-TO

never nunca NOON-KAH

newspaper periódico (m) PA-BEE-O-DEE-KO

newstand quiosco de periódicos (m) KEE-OS-KO DA
  PE-BEE-O-DEE-KOS

next time la próxima LAH PBOK-SEE-MAH

night noche (f) NO-CHA

nightclub cabaret (m) KAH-BAH-BET

no no NO

no smoking no fumar NO FOO-MAHB

noon mediodía (m) MA-DEE-O-DEE-AH

north norte (m) NOB-TA

notary notario (m) NO-TAH-BEE-O

November noviembre (m) NO-VEE-EM-BBA

now ahora AH-O-BAH

number número (m) NOO-MA-BO

nurse enfermera (f) EN-FEB-MA-BAH

O

occupied ocupado Ⓞ-Kⓞⓞ-Pⓐ́-Dⓞ
ocean océano Ⓞ-Sⓐ́-ⓐ-Nⓞ
October octubre (m) ⓄK-Tⓞⓞ-BⓇⓐ
officer oficial (m) Ⓞ-Fⓔⓔ-Sⓔⓔ-ⓐL
oil aceite (m) ⓐ-Sⓐ́-Tⓐ
omelet tortilla de huevos (f)
　　TⓄⓇ-Tⓔⓔ-Yⓐ Dⓐ Wⓐ́-VⓞS
one way (traffic) una vía. un solo sentido
　　ⓞⓞ-Nⓐ Vⓔⓔ-ⓐ, ⓞⓞN SⓄ́-Lⓞ Sⓔ́N-Tⓔⓔ-Dⓞ
onion cebolla (f) Sⓐ-Bⓞ́-Yⓐ
open (to) abrir ⓐ-BⓇⓔⓔR
opera ópera (f) Ⓞ́-Pⓐ-Rⓐ
operator operadora (f) Ⓞ-Pⓐ-Rⓐ-Dⓞ́R-ⓐ
optician optometrista (m) ⓄP-Tⓞ-Mⓐ-TⓇⓔⓔ́S-Tⓐ
orange (color) anaranjado ⓐ-Nⓐ-Rⓐ́N-Hⓐ́-Dⓞ
orange (fruit) naranja (f) Nⓐ-Rⓐ́N-Hⓐ
order (to) pedir Pⓐ-DⓔⓔR
original original Ⓞ-Rⓔⓔ-Hⓔⓔ-Nⓐ́L
owner dueño (m) DWⓐN-Yⓞ
oysters ostras (f) Ⓞ́S-TRⓐS

P

package paquete (m) Pⓐ-Kⓐ́-Tⓐ
paid pagado Pⓐ-Gⓐ́-Dⓞ
pain dolor (m) Dⓞ-Lⓞ́R
painting pintura (f) PⓔⓔN-Tⓞⓞ-Rⓐ
pantyhose pantimedias (f/pl) PⓐN-Tⓔⓔ-Mⓐ́-Dⓔⓔ-ⓐS
paper papel (m) Pⓐ-Pⓔ́L
park parque (m) Pⓐ́R-Kⓐ
park (to) estacionarse ⓐ-STⓐ-Sⓔⓔ-Ⓞ-NⓐⓇ-Sⓐ
partner (business) socio (m) SⓄ́-Sⓔⓔ-Ⓞ
party fiesta (f) Fⓔⓔ-ⓔ́S-Tⓐ

passenger pasajero (m) Pah-Sah-HÁ-RO

passport pasaporte (m) Pah-Sah-PÓR-TA

pasta pasta PáhS-Tah

pastry pastel (m) Pah-STêL

pen pluma (f) PLoo-Mah

pencil lápiz (m) Láh-PeeS

pepper pimienta (f) Pee-Mee-êN-Tah

perfume perfume (m) PêR-Foo-MA

person persona (f) PêR-SÓ-Nah

person to person persona a persona
     PêR-SÓ-Nah A PêR-SÓ-Nah

pharmacist farmacéutico (m) Fah-Mah-Soo-TEE-KO

pharmacy farmacia (f) Fah-Máh-SEE-ah

phone book guía telefónica (f)
     Gee-ah TA-LA-FO-Nee-Kah

photo foto (f) FÓ-TO

photographer fotógrafo (m) FO-TÓ-GRah-FO

pie (follow with name of filling) pastel de (m) Pah-STêL DA

pillow almohada (f) ahL-MO-ah-Dah

pink rosado RO-Sah-DO

pizza pizza (f) PEET-Sah or PEE-Sah

plastic plástico (m) PLáhS-TEE-KO

plate plato (m) PLah-TO

please por favor POR Fah-VÓR

pleasure placer (m) PLah-SêR

police policía (f) PO-LEE-SEE-ah

police station comisaría (f) KO-Mee-Sah-REE-ah

pork carne de puerco (f) Káh R-NA DA PWêR-KO

porter maletero (m) Mah-LA-TÁ-RO

post office el correo (m) êL KO-RÁ-O

postcard tarjeta postal (f) Tah R-HÁ-Tah POS-Tah L

potato papa (f), patata (f) (Spain) Pah-Pah, Pah-Táh-Tah

pregnant embarazada ⓔM-Bⓐⓗ-Rⓐⓗ-Sⓐⓗ-Dⓐⓗ
prescription receta (f) Rⓐ-Sⓐ́-Tⓐⓗ
price precio (m) PRⓐ́-Sⓔⓔ-Ⓞ
problem problema (m) PRⓄ-BLⓐ́-Mⓐⓗ
profession profesión (f) PRⓄ-Fⓐ-Sⓔⓔ-Ⓞ́N
public público PⓄⓄB-Lⓔⓔ-KⓄ
public telephone teléfono público (m)
    Tⓐ-Lⓐ́-FⓄ-NⓄ PⓄⓄB-Lⓔⓔ-KⓄ
purified purificada PⓄⓄ-Rⓔⓔ-Fⓔⓔ-Cⓐⓗ-Dⓐⓗ
purple morado MⓄ-Rⓐⓗ́-DⓄ
purse bolsa (f) BⓄ́L-Sⓐⓗ
Q
quality calidad (f) Kⓐⓗ-Lⓔⓔ-Dⓐⓗ́D
question pregunta (f) PRⓐ-GⓄⓄN-Tⓐⓗ
quickly rápido Rⓐⓗ́-Pⓔⓔ-DⓄ
quiet callado Kⓐⓗ-Yⓐⓗ́-DⓄ
quiet!, be ¡silencio! Sⓔⓔ-Lⓔ́N-Sⓔⓔ-Ⓞ
R
radio radio (f) Rⓐⓗ-Dⓔⓔ-Ⓞ
railroad ferrocarril (m) Fⓐ-RⓄ-Kⓐⓗ-Rⓔ́L
rain lluvia (f) YⓄⓄ-Vⓔⓔ-ⓐⓗ
raincoat impermeable (m) ⓔM-Pⓔ́R-Mⓐ-ⓐⓗ-BLⓐ
ramp rampa (f) RⓐⓗM-Pⓐⓗ
rare (cooked) poco cocida PⓄ́-KⓄ KⓄ-Sⓔ́-Dⓐⓗ
razor blades hojas de afeitar (f/pl)
    Ⓞ́-HⓐⓗS Dⓐ ⓐⓗ-Fⓐ-Tⓐⓗ́R
ready listo (m), lista (f) Lⓔ́S-TⓄ, Lⓔ́S-Tⓐⓗ
receipt recibo (m) Rⓐ-Sⓔ́-BⓄ
recommend (to) recomendar Rⓐ-KⓄ-MⓔN-Dⓐⓗ́R
red rojo RⓄ́-HⓄ
repeat! ¡repita! Rⓐ-Pⓔ́-Tⓐⓗ

reservation reservación (f) RA-SER-Vah-SEE-ON
restaurant restaurante (m) RES-Tow-RahN-TA
return (to) (a thing) devolver DA-VOL-VER
    (a person) volver VOL-VER
rice arroz (m) ah-ROS
rich rico REE-KO
right (correct) correcto KO-REK-TO
right (direction) derecha DA-RA-CHah
road camino (m) Kah-MEE-NO
room cuarto (m) KWah-R-TO
round trip ida y vuelta EE-Dah EE VWEL-Tah
S
safe (in a hotel) caja fuerte (f) Kah-Hah FWER-TA
salad ensalada (f) EN-Sah-Lah-Dah
sale venta (f) VEN-Tah
salmon salmón (m) Sah-L-MON
salt sal (f) SahL
sandwich torta (f) TOR-Tah
        bocadillo (m) (Spain) BO-Kah-DEE-YO
Saturday sábado (m) Sah-Bah-DO
scissors tijeras (f) TEE-HA-RahS
sculpture escultura (f) ES-Koo-L-Too-Rah
seafood mariscos, (m/plural) Mah-REES-KOS
season estación (f) ES-Tah-SEE-ON
seat asiento (m) ah-SEE-EN-TO
secretary secretaria (f) SA-KRA-Tah-REE-ah
section sección (f) SEK-SEE-ON
September septiembre (m) SEP-TEE-EM-BRA
service servicio (m) SER-VEE-SEE-O
several varios Vah-REE-OS
shampoo champú (m) CHahM-Poo
sheets, bed sábanas (f/pl) Sah-Bah-NahS

shirt camisa (f) Kah-MEE-Sah

shoes zapatos (m/pl) Sah-Pah-TOS

shoe store zapatería (f) Sah-Pah-TA-REE-ah

shop tienda (f) TEE-EN-Dah

shopping center centro comercial (m)
    SEN-TRO KO-MER-SEE-ahL

shower ducha (f) Doo-CHah

shrimp camarones (m/pl) Kah-Mah-RO-NES

sick enfermo (m) EN-FER-MO

sign (display) letrero (m) LA-TRA-RO

signature firma (f) FEER-Mah

silence! ¡silencio! SEE-LEN-SEE-O

single solo SO-LO

sir señor (m) SAN-YOR

sister hermana (f) ER-Mah-Nah

size tamaño (m) Tah-MahN-YO, medida (f) MA-DEE-Dah

skin piel (f) PEE-EL

skirt falda (f) FahL-Dah

sleeve manga (f) MahN-Gah

slowly despacio DA-SPah-SEE-O

small (amount) poquito PO-KEE-TO

small (size) pequeño PA-KAN-YO

smile (to) sonreír SON-RA-EER

smoke (to) fumar Foo-MahR

soap jabón (m) Hah-BON

socks calcetas (f/pl) KahL-SA-Tahs
    calcetines (m)   KahL-SA-TEE-NES

some unos (m/pl), unas (f/pl) oo-NOS, oo-NahS
    algunos, algunas (w/numbers) ahL-GO-NOS, ahL-Goo-NahS

something algo ahL-GO

sometimes algunas veces ahL-Goo-NahS VA-SES

soon pronto PRON-TO

sorry, I am lo siento LO SEE-EN-TO

soup sopa (f), caldo (m) SO-Pah, KahL-DO

south sur (m) SOOR

souvenir recuerdo (m) Rah-KWER-DO

Spanish español (m) eS-Pah-N-YOL

    castellanol (m) CahS-TA-Yah-NO

speciality especial A-SPA-SEE-ahL

speed velocidad (f) VA-LO-SEE-DahD

spoon cuchara (f) KOO-CHah-Rah

sport deporte (m) DA-POR-TA

spring (season) primavera (f) PREE-Mah-VA-Rah

stairs escalera (f) AS-Kah-LA-Rah

stamp sello (m), timbre (m) SA-YO, TEM-BRA

station estación (f) eS-Tah-SEE-ON

steak bistec (m) BEE-STEK

steamed cocido por vapor KO-SEE-DO POR Vah-POR

stop! ¡pare! Pah-RA

store tienda (f) TEE-eN-Dah

storm tormenta (f) TOR-MeN-Tah

straight ahead derecho DA-RA-CHO

strawberry fresa (f) FRA-Sah

street calle (f) Kah-YA

string cuerda (f) KWER-Dah

subway metro (m) MA-TRO

    subterráneo (m) (Spain) SOOR-TA-Rah-NA-O

sugar azúcar (f) ah-SOO-KahR

suit (clothes) traje (m) TRah-HA

suitcase maleta (f) Mah-LA-Tah

summer verano (m) VE-Rah-NO

sun sol (m) SOL
sun tan lotion loción bronceador (f)
　　LO-SEE-ON BRON-SA-ah-DOR
Sunday domingo (m) DO-MEEN-GO
sunglasses lentes de sol (f/pl) LEN-TES DA SOL
supermarket supermercado (m) Soo-PER-MER-Kah-DO
surprise sorpresa (f) SOR-PRA-Sah
sweet dulce DooL-SA
swim (to) nadar Nah-DAR
swimming pool piscina (f) PEE-SEE-Nah
　　alberca (f) ahL-BER-Kah
synagogue sinagoga (f) SEEN-ah-GO-Gah
T
table mesa (f) MA-Sah
tampons tampones (m), absorbentes higiénicos (m)
　　TahM-PO-NES, ah-SOR-BEN-TES EE-HEE-E-NEE-KOS
tape (sticky) cinta (f) SEEN-Tah
tape recorder grabador (m) GRah-Bah-DOR
tax impuesto (m) EEM-PWAS-TO
taxi taxi (m) TahK-SEE
tea té (m) TA
telegram telegrama (m) TA-LA-GRah-Mah
telephone teléfono (m) TA-LA-FO-NO
television televisión (f) TA-LA-VEE-SEE-ON
temperature temperatura (f) TEM-PA-Rah-Too-Rah
temple templo (m) TEM-PLO
tennis tenis (m) TE-NEES
tennis court cancha de tenís (f)
　　KahN-CHah DA TA-NEES
thank you gracias GRah-SEE-ahS
that ese (m), esa (f) E-SA, E-Sah

the el (m), la (f), los (m/pl), las (f/pl) ⓔL, Lⓐh, LⓄS, LⓐhS
theater teatro (m) Tⓐ-ah'-TRⓄ
there allí, ahí ahⒽ-YⒺ, ahⒽ-ⒺⒺ
they ellos (m/pl), ellas (f/pl) Ⓐ-YⓄS, Ⓐ'-YahⓈ
this este ⓔS-Tⓐ
thread hilo (m) ⒺⒺ'-LⓄ
throat garganta (f) GahR-Gah'N-Tah
Thursday jueves (m) HWⒶ'-VⓔS
ticket billete (m), boleto (m) BⒺⒺ-Yⓔ'-Tⓐ, BⓄ-Lⓐ'-TⓄ
tie corbata (f) KⓄR-Bah'-Tah
time tiempo (m) TⒺⒺ-ⓔ'M-PⓄ, hora (f) ⓄⓇ-RⓐhH
tip (gratuity) propina (f) PRⓄ-PⒺⒺ-Nah
tire llanta (f) Yah'N-Tah
tired cansado KahN-Sah'-DⓄ
toast pan tostado (m) PahN TⓄ-STah'-DⓄ
tobacco tabaco (m) Tah-Bah'-KⓄ
today hoy ⓄY
toe dedo del pie (m) Dⓐ'-DⓄ DⓔL PⒺⒺ-Ⓐ
together juntos HⓄⓄN-TⓄS
toilet baño (m) Bah'N-YⓄ
toilet paper papel higiénico (m) Pah-Pⓔ'L Ⓔ-HⒺⒺ-ⓔ'-ⒺⒺ-KⓄ
tomato tomate (m) TⓄ-Mah'-Tⓐ
    jitomate (m) HⒺⒺ-TⓄ-Mah'-Tⓐ
tomorrow mañana MahN-Yah'-Nah
tooth ache dolor de dientes (f)
    DⓄ-LⓄ'R Dⓐ DⒺⒺ-ⓔ'N-TⓔS
toothbrush cepillo de dientes (m)
    Sⓐ-PⒺⒺ'-YⓄ Dⓐ DⒺⒺ-ⓔ'N-TⓔS
toothpaste pasta de dientes (f)
    Pah'S-Tah Dⓐ DⒺⒺ-ⓔ'N-TⓔS
toothpick palillo (m) Pah-LⒺⒺ'-YⓄ

tour excursión (f) EKS-KooR-SEE-ON
tourist turista (m&f) Too-REES-Tah
tourist office oficina de turismo (f)
  O-FEE-SEE-Nah DA Too-REEZ-MO
towel toalla (f) TO-ah-Yah
train tren (m) TREN
travel agency agencia de viajes (m)
  ah-HEN-SEE-A DA VEE-ah-HAS
traveler's check cheque de viajero (m)
  CHA-KA DA VEE-ah-HA-RO
trip viaje (m) VEE-ah-HA
trousers pantalones (m) PahN-Tah-LO-NES
trout trucha (f) TRoo-CHah
truth verdad (f) VER-DahD
Tuesday martes (m) MahR-TES
turkey pavo (m) Pah-VO
  guajolote (m) (Mexico) GWah-HO-LO-TA
U
umbrella paraguas (m) Pah-Rah-GWahS
understand (to) entender EN-TEN-DER
underwear ropa interior (f) RO-Pah EN-TE-REE-OR
United States Estados Unidos (m/pl)
  ES-Tah-DOS oo-NEE-DOS
university universidad (f) oo-NEE-VER-SEE-DahD
up arriba ah-REE-Bah
urgent urgente ooR-HEN-TA
V
vacancies (accommodation) habitación libre
  ah-BEE-Tah-SEE-ON LEE-BRA
vacant desocupado DA-SO-Koo-Pah-DO
vacation vacación (f) Vah-Kah-SEE-ON

valuable precioso   PRA-SEE-O-SO
value valor (m)   Vah-LOR
vanilla vainilla (f)   VI-NEE-Yah
veal carne de ternera (f)   Kah'R-NA DA TER-NA-Rah
vegetables legumbres (f/pl), vegetales (f/pl)
     LA-GOOM-BRES, VE-HA-Tah-LES
view vista (f)   VEES-Tah
vinegar vinagre (m)   VEE-Nah-GRA
voyage viaje (m)   VEE-ah-HA
W
wait! ¡espérese!   ES-PA-RA-SA
waiter camarero (m)   Kah-Mah-RA-RO
     mozo (m) (Spain)   MO-THO
waitress camarera (f)   Kah-Mah-RA-Rah
     moza (Spain) (f)   MO-THah
want, I quiero   KEE-E-RO
wash (to) lavar   Lah-Vah'R
watch (time piece) reloj (m)   RE-LOH
watch out! ¡Cuidado!   KWEE-Dah-DO
water agua (m)   ah-GWah
watermelon sandia (f)   SahN-DEE-ah
we nosotros (m/pl)   NO-SO-TROS
weather tiempo (m)   TEE-EM-PO
Wednesday miércoles (m)   MEE-ER-KO-LES
week semana (f)   SA-Mah-Nah
weekend fin de semana (m)   FEEN DA SA-Mah'N-ah
welcome ¡bienvenido!   BEE-EN-VA-NEE-DO
well done (cooked) bien cocida   BEE-EN KO-SEE-Dah
west oeste (m)   O-ES-TA
what? ¿qué? KA, ¿cómo? KO-MO
wheelchair silla de ruedas (f)   SEE-Yah DA ROO-A-DahS

when cuándo KWⓐN-DⓄ

where dónde DⓄN-DⒶ

which cuál KWⓐL

white blanco BLⓐhN-KⓄ

who quién KⒺ-ⒺN

why? ¿por qué? PⓄB-KⒶ?

wife esposa (f) ⒺS-PⓄ-Sⓐh

wind viento (m) VⒺ-ⒺN-TⓄ

window ventana (f) VⒺN-Tⓐh-Nⓐh

wine list lista de vinos (f) LⒺS-Tⓐh DⒶ VⒺ-NⓄS

wine vino (m) VⒺ-NⓄ

winter invierno (m) ⒺN-VⒺ-ⒺB-NⓄ

with con KⓄN

woman mujer (f) Mⓞⓞ-HⒺB

wonderful maravilloso Mⓐh-Bⓐh-VⒺ-YⓄ-SⓄ

world mundo (m) MⓞⓞN-DⓄ

wrong equivocado, incorrecto

Ⓐ-KⒺ-VⓄ-Kⓐh-DⓄ, ⒺN-KⓄ-BⒺK-TⓄ

XYZ

year año (m) ⓐhN-YⓄ

yellow amarillo ⓐh-Mⓐh-BⒺ-YⓄ

yes sí SⒺ

yesterday ayer ⓐh-YⒺB

you usted (formal), tú (informal) ⓞⓞ-STⒺD, Tⓞⓞ

zipper cierre (m) SⒺ-Ⓔ-BⒶ

zoo zoológico (m) SⓄⓄ-LⓄ-HⒺ-KⓄ

INDEX

CAN NOT FIND THESE OTHER EASY TO PRONOUNCE LANGUAGE PHRASE BOOKS ?

THEN RETURN THIS ORDER TO:

GRIFFIN PUBLISHING
544 W. COLORADO STREET
GLENDALE, CALIFORNIA 91204
800 826-4849 NATIONAL
800 423-5789 IN CALIFORNIA

NAME:_____

ADDRESS:_____

CITY:_____STATE: _____

ZIP:_____PHONE:_____

	QTY	@ PRICE	TOTAL
ENGLISH to SPANISH	_____	$7.95	_____
ENGLISH to FRENCH	_____	$7.95	_____
ENGLISH to GERMAN	_____	$7.95	_____
ENGLISH to ITALIAN	_____	$7.95	_____
ENGLISH to JAPANESE	_____	$7.95	_____
SUB-TOTALS	_____		_____
SHIPPING INCLUDED			
SALES TAX 8.25%			_____
TOTAL			_____

CHECK/MONEY ORDER AMOUNT INCLUDED   _____

CREDIT CARD #_____

EXP. DATE_____

SIGNATURE_____